our cousin

24

SHAKESPEARE'S PRODUCING HAND

*A Study of his Marks of Expression
to be found in the First Folio*

BY

RICHARD FLATTER

His mind and hand went together:
IOHN HEMINGE
HENRIE CONDELL

NEW YORK
W · W · NORTON & COMPANY · INC ·

First Edition

CONTENTS

ILLUSTRATIONS

INTRODUCTION

DR. FLATTER'S book seems to me the next great step forward in the detailed interpretation of Shakespeare's stagecraft since the *Prefaces* of the late Harley Granville Barker, whose death cut short a work in that field which Bradley had begun. By his perception of the nuances of character, atmosphere and philosophical currents, Bradley's great work did all that could be done by a Shakespearian scholar in the study. Granville Barker brought to that kind of knowledge the added powers of a man of theatre who was also a man of genius. He was the greatest Shakespearian producer of our century, and his written studies of so many (alas, not all) of Shakespeare's plays confirm this.

In a letter he wrote me shortly before his death, Granville Barker wrote:

. . . "But it would take fifty years—two or three generations of actors moulding a tradition—to develop a performance, which *should* please us both. That is going to be my gospel now . . . QUALITY. The fruits of the past fifty years are now ready to be picked; Quantity. When I started, you could not get plays *done;* and when they were . . . oh, Lord . . ."

In this book of Dr. Flatter's a new field of enquiry, out of which a rich harvest of that *Quality* is ready for reaping, has been discerned and opened to all lovers of Shakespeare's theatrical subtlety and vision. The author is not only a distinguished translator of Shakespeare and a close scholar of the best texts, but also a man of theatre, trained under Max Reinhardt. In my opinion, no producer, actor or editor who himself aims at distinction in Shakespearian work can afford to ignore Dr. Flatter's revolutionary discoveries, and the large general public that is daily growing in Shakespearian enthusiasm and discernment will, I think, also find and delight in the subtle accents and flashes of illumination revealed by his study and the method or principles on which he has based it.

It has long been thought, and to a large extent established, that the text of the First Folio of 1623 and the "Good" Quartos of Shakespeare was probably printed from Shakespeare's autograph, now lost. Dr. Flatter has examined this view seriously by pondering upon the telling details, hitherto unremarked, noting the verse-pauses and peculiarities of punctuation that were once brushed aside as the work of ignorant compositors. The results of his investigation are astonishing and, I think, in almost every case authoritative and convincing.

Did Shakespeare bother about his punctuation? One has only to hear the mess made by Quince of his Prologue to the lamentable comedy of Pyramus and Thisbe with the ears of Duke Theseus and his courtiers . . .

> His speech was like a tangled chain, nothing
> impaired but all disordered

. . . to know that Shakespeare well knew the value of a comma.

Dr. Flatter has revealed how a comma, and other such seeming trifles, when placed there by Shakespeare's hand, are often direct and intelligible directions to actors and producers. No one has fully seen this point before. Those who will give themselves the pleasure of following Dr. Flatter's arguments (for they are as lucid as they are persuasive) will find in them a new and exciting way of discovering some of that *Quality* of which Granville Barker wrote and which it now appears from this essay Shakespeare intended.

There may be much that is controversial in this book. But the rightness and richness of this new approach to problems of dramatic interpretation seem to me absolutely established here. Though it is a book that has a special interest for actors and producers, it has much in it for every lover of Shakespeare.

NEVILL COGHILL,
Exeter College, Oxford.

FOREWORD

MANY a book has been written *On Reading Shakespeare*, no matter whether or no that title has been actually used; yet so far no book has been written *On Writing Shakespeare*. My own approach to Shakespeare has been that of writing him—to which I hasten to add that by "writing Shakespeare" I mean copying his texts or, still more precisely, translating them. Nevertheless it will be seen that the technical process of writing has in my case not been without consequence.

On a certain occasion some time ago I asked a friend of mine, a Shakespeare scholar, whether he had ever happened to write out in his own hand a single play of Shakespeare's. "No", he replied, "why should I?" Exactly: why should he? Not even for an editor of the plays is there any need nowadays to copy the texts himself. In my case it has been different. So far I have translated into German (in addition to the *Sonnets*) eighteen of the plays; in doing so I had to write them down in my own hand, and not once, but three and four times. First in shorthand: the first draft, line by line; then in longhand: to enable me to read the passage easily and as a whole, and to make more corrections and alterations; then I had to make a fair copy and, finally, since I had to act also as editor of the plays as far as they have been printed, to read the proofs.

Now, a copyist who for years on end is busy copying Rembrandt's large pictures is bound gradually to develop some measure of familiarity with his master's technique. He will find out his peculiarities in mixing the colours, his

I

method of applying them, his tricks of perspective, and so on: he will as it were detect his finger-prints. In the same way, if by nothing else but the technical process of copying him, I could hardly fail to learn something about my own master's technicalities, his versification, punctuation, rhythm, and so forth—and in this book I propose to submit what I have found: things that I think are distinctive features of Shakespeare's peculiar diction: the hall-marks, so to speak, of his forge.

First, however, it might be useful to give a few instances of the problems I found myself confronted with at every turn.

(1)

When in *Twelfth-Night*, I. 2. 44, I came across a line with only four syllables, a line not continued by the next speaker, who instead starts a line of her own:

Captain: Because she will admit no kind of suit,
          No, not the duke's.
Viola: There is a fair behaviour in thee, captain . . .

—what was I to do? Was I to fill in the gap after "duke's", making the translation of the Captain's last words a little longer? Or was I to let Viola start in the middle of the next line, thus continuing the Captain's verse? Was it Shakespeare's intention to interrupt the continuous flow of his iambics? Why should he deviate in this case from his normal way of letting the second character continue the verse broken off by the first? Is the irregularity of the Captain's line a slip of the pen, or is there any meaning behind it?

Schlegel, while rendering the passage, was obviously of the opinion that the irregularity was not intended: he made the Captain's speech longer (a thing very easily done in German) so that the line became a regular iambus with ten syllables. Was Schlegel right? I wondered.

(2)

In *Romeo and Juliet*, II. 3, Friar Laurence enters with the words:

The grey-ey'd morn smiles on the frowning night . . .
x — x — / — x x — x —

The words "morn" and "smiles", both of them stressed, stand side by side, no unstressed syllable between them. The result is that "morn" must be held a little longer, just long enough to bridge over the following gap caused by the missing syllable—with the further result that "smiles on the" becomes a dactyl. Thus, together with the harmony of the two contrasting long vowels in "morn" and "smiles", an exquisitely musical effect is achieved by the simple means of that "irregularity" in the versification.

Schlegel to whom I turned failed me once more. He, unfortunately, translated not only Friar Laurence's soliloquy but also the ensuing dialogue between the Friar and Romeo in Alexandrines. That has been corrected by later editors of his texts who cut the Alexandrines down to iambic length (a cruel process by which the lines were scarcely improved); but none of those editors either saw or followed the rhythm of that first line. And yet I was unable to persuade myself that so magnificent a line should owe its rhythmical beauty to chance or negligence or to the author's lack of efficiency in writing verse. In my own text I copied the rhythm.

(3)

Ophelia, in II. 1. 77 ff., concludes her report on Hamlet's visit:

My lord, as I was sewing in my chamber . . .

with the line:

To speak of horrors: he comes before me.

(The colon is the punctuation of the Folio.) In the middle of the line one syllable, a stressed one, is missing:

$$x - x - x (-) x - x - x$$

Again the question arises: is the translator to regularize the line by inserting the missing syllable? Or ought he to imitate the gap? It is in fine the same problem as before: whether the "irregularity" is due to chance or intention.

Turning to Schlegel I found that he either did not notice the gap in the verse or else regarded the line as faulty: in any case he made his translation of the line a regular and complete iambus. I did not think fit to follow his example: in my text the line shows the same gap, the third stress being omitted.

(4)

In *Hamlet*, I. I. 35 ff. the structure is irregular in that the sentence has no verb:

Last night of all,
When yond same star that's westward from the pole
Had made his course t'illume that part of heaven
Where now it burns, Marcellus and myself,
The bell then beating one—

Marc.:   Peace, break thee off!
            (*Enter the Ghost.*)

Here, too, Schlegel deemed it necessary to correct his author: he inserted the verb by adding: "*da sahn* Marcell und ich". But is it impossible to assume that Shakespeare

4

made the omission on purpose? that it was his aim thus to heighten the uncanny suspense of the situation? Once more the question obtrudes itself: is the translator permitted to insert what the poet—perhaps—was careful to omit? In my translation the verb is missing.

(5)

In *Othello*, I. I. 107, Roderigo replies to Brabantio, whom he and Iago have roused from his sleep:

> Most grave Brabantio,
> In simple and pure soul I come to you.

This is how the line appears in all modern editions. It does not seem to be clear, and the German translations make no sense at all, because their authors did not turn to the Folio for consultation. Yet if we do we find first of all a comma after "soul"; also we ought to remember that in the Folio a full stop often stands for what in modern punctuation would be a dash. The line, then, printed as it ought to be printed:

> In simple and pure soul, I come to you—

has the meaning: "Plainly and honestly speaking, I have come to you (to tell you . . .)"—whereupon Iago, impatient of the bungling of this simple soul, interrupts him: "Zounds, sir, you are one of those . . .". Thus I was able to get sense into the translation.

(6)

The English editor of the plays has to deal with line-division, punctuation, stage-directions, and a few minor

5   B

points. But should he come across a passage the meaning of which is difficult to grasp, it is not his office to interfere with the text. Only in a foot-note or in an Appendix may he give an explanation.

For the translator no such thing as an unintelligible passage is allowed to exist. He cannot (at least he should not) translate a single sentence unless he understands it. Nor ought he to shirk his task by rendering the passage verbatim, thus palming off his own shortcomings as Shakespeare's.

In *King Lear*, IV. i. 10 ff., Edgar recognizes his blind father and exclaims:

> World, world, O world!
> But that thy strange mutations make us hate thee,
> Life would not yield to age.

The sentence seems to contain a self-contradiction: "Life would not yield to age", i.e. we should not allow ourselves to grow old, if "thy strange mutations would not make us hate thee". We should expect the contrary, something like: "if thy strange mutations would not reconcile us with thee". Furness, in his *Variorum Edition*, quotes three attempts at explanation, none of them satisfactory; the paraphrases given by the *New Hudson*, by *The Arden Shakespeare*, and others are of no help. The German versions do not throw any light on the matter either: they give verbal translations which are unintelligible.

The crucial words are "strange mutations". All commentators identify them with the "lamentable change" of which Edgar speaks a few lines earlier. This I think is misleading; there is no connection between the two passages. What Edgar has in mind is not "reverses of fortune and changes such as I now see and feel" (Malone); nor is it "the changes and calamitous reverses which the years

6

bring" (*New Hudson*). W. J. Craig (*The Arden Shake-speare*) gives the following paraphrase:

> If the mutations of the world did not give us the spirit of detachment, we could not endure the stress and strain of life. Being detached from the world, hating it, we can bear its mutations with a certain stoical equanimity.

This seems to be a fantasia more than a paraphrase.

What Edgar thinks of, as I understand the passage, is not changes during, but after, life. The "strange mutations" are the transformations that happen to us when we die or are dead. Paraphrased the passage would read:

> O world, were it not for those strange transformations (after death, which thou bringest about and) for which we hate thee, we should never consent to become old.

The thought is genuine Shakespeare. Claudio in *Measure for Measure* expresses it:

> Ay, but to die, and go we know not where;
> To lie in cold obstruction and to rot . . .

and Hamlet, in the Graveyard-scene, speculates on the noble dust of Alexander, stopping a bung-hole:

> To what base uses we may return, Horatio!

In my opinion it is the "dread of something after death" of which Edgar speaks. In this sense at least I have translated his words.

(7)

Another problem the translator has to deal with arises where the text of one play has come down to us not only

7

in the Folio but also in a Quarto edition. In such a case
he is confronted with the question which version he is to
regard as the better authority. The following lines from
Othello (I. 3. 261 ff.) are perhaps a good example. Desdemona asks permission to accompany her husband. In the
Folio the passage reads:

> By his deere absence. Let me go with him.
> *Othe.:* Let her haue your voice.
>   Vouch with me Heauen, I therefore beg it not . . .

In the Quarto, however, published the year before the
Folio, the passage reads as follows:

> By your deare absence, let me goe with him.
> *Oth.:* Your voyces Lords: beseech you let her will,
>   Haue a free way, I therefore beg it not . . .

Which way has one to turn? The modern editors are
not unanimous; some have decided for the Folio, some for
the Quarto, and Dyce has both versions:

> Your voices, lords: beseech you, let her will
> Have a free way.
> Vouch with me, heaven, I therefore beg it not . . .

I have chosen the Folio version, and for these reasons:
Othello, in his naïve and simple way, first contents himself with adding a few words only to his wife's request:

> Let her have your voice.

Then, however, looking round, he notices with alarm that
the Magnificoes are not going to agree. To permit a
general when he goes to the wars to take his newly-
married wife with him? Impossible. Seeing their un-
favourable attitude Othello starts pleading in earnest and
with vehemence (using up fourteen lines)—but not before
that short pause of his looking round and their showing
disapproval, a pause which the author himself indicates:

8

by making that gap in the versification after "voice".

It was evidently that gap that irritated the man who "edited" the Quarto 1622. He failed to understand the theatrical meaning of that break in verse, and so, bent on "regular" versification, he altered the text as he thought fit, so as to fill in that gap. To assume that it was Shakespeare himself who, having an "afterthought", obliterated so telling and necessary a pause would be contrary to his policy of pauses of which we have so many instances throughout the later plays.

*

Why have I given those examples?

In the first place I wish to expose the fallacy, still widely held, that any translation of Shakespeare, even a version as magnificent as Schlegel's, could ever bear comparison with the original. Of translations the words of Leonard Digges will always be true; himself a translator (from the Spanish) and author of a poem, inserted in the First Folio, in praise of "the deceased Authour Maister W. Shakepeare", Digges says:

> Translations (as says a witty Spaniard) are, in respect of their originals, like the knotty wrong-side of arras-hangings.

My chief aim, however, in giving those illustrations has been to describe my special approach to Shakespeare; for it is due to the technical handling of his texts more than to anything else that certain aspects of his diction have appeared to me to fall into a kind of system. I cannot claim to have made any discovery; those things have of course been known for long. But a broken-off verse, a missing syllable, an irregular stress, etc., must to the man who merely reads the lines seem less significant than to him who has to rewrite them and who, in doing so, is compelled to ask himself over and over again whether he does not fail in his duty if his version does not reproduce those irregular features. Having put that question to myself on innumerable occasions I have in the end found out—or at least I think so—that certain peculiarities of diction are more often than not attributable to certain reasons: certain means are used for certain artistic purposes.

Anticipating the results I may say that certainly not all, but undoubtedly most, of those "irregularities" in Shakespeare's diction are due to his art as actor or, to use modern parlance, his art as producer. They are the outcome, and incidentally the proof, of his eminent ingenuity in performing not only his own part but each of the parts, in fact the whole play. Those "irregularities" amount to stage-directions, wrought into the text itself.

In this connection I feel I have to add that I am a pupil of Max Reinhardt. A translator of Shakespeare, I thought, cannot allow himself not to be in touch with the living stage. Taking advantage, therefore, of the fact that Reinhardt at that time had a theatrical seminary in my native city Vienna, I went and studied stage-production for two years. That probably accounts for the tendency I have acquired to look at Shakespeare's texts as though from the prompter's corner and to scrutinize them for the producer's thumb-marks.

Unfortunately, many of these thumb-marks have been erased by the editors. The india-rubber, used by Rowe, Pope, and others, has had a deplorable effect. They thought it their duty to regularize "irregular" rhythms, to correct "faulty" lines, and to put in order "ungrammatical" punctuation. By doing so they obliterated hints, pointers, and signposts that the producer was so careful to insert. It will take a hundred years to purge the editions of those "corrections". The worst, however, happened when the editors put aside the india-rubber and used scissors and paste instead, i.e. when they interfered with the line-division, cutting off part of a verse here and pasting it to another verse there. In this way they have spoiled the rhythm of the passages affected—often of whole scenes, especially in *Macbeth*—and made unrecognizable what might be called implied stage-directions.

The farther I proceeded with my work of translation the more I became conscious of the extent to which the "True Originall Copies" are superior to the subsequent editions. It is true that the First Folio contains a great number of misprints; but as far as punctuation, line-division, and other signs and imprints of the producer's activities go, I found myself frequently misguided by what the modern editors have done. On many occasions, endeavouring to find out what Shakespeare really meant and said and how he said it, I had to turn to the Folio —and in most cases I was amply rewarded.

It would, no doubt, be considerable imprudence in a foreigner to dare an intrusion into the field of Shakespeare's diction; the fact, however, that my approach, that of a translator, is a singular one may be considered —at least I hope so—to be sufficient ground on which to base my apology for the venture of this book.

I

"ASIDE"

In *Hamlet*, IV. 5. 98:

King: What is the matter?
Gentl.:   Save yourself, my lord. . . .

or in *A Midsummer-Night's Dream*, II. 1. 42:

Fairy: Are you not he?
Puck: Fairy, thou speak'st aright. . . .

the replies continue the verse started by the first character. In the case of lines unfinished by the speaker, that kind of line-division appears to be the rule wherever two persons answer each other or are otherwise engaged in unbroken conversation. Continued verse signifies continued dialogue.

If that is so, are we, by the logic of conversion, justified in expecting that a speaker who, either by failing to answer or in any other way, does not continue the dialogue would discontinue the verse also? In such a case the second speaker would disregard the line broken off by the first; by starting a line of his own he would cause a break in the flow of versification. Are we, then, to assume that a break in versification means discontinuation of the dialogue?

Conversation and, accordingly, versification can be broken in various ways; yet most of the breaks are due to one of the following three causes:

(a) the "aside", when the subsequent speaker is supposed not to have heard what the first speaker said;

(b) deliberate pause in dialogue, when one of the characters stops for a while before continuing or re-starting his own speech, and

(c) simultaneous speech, when one speaker interferes with the other's speech, but without interrupting him.

Taking the "aside" first, I propose, before turning to Shakespeare, to examine the way in which others deal with it as far as versification is concerned.

In John Ford's tragedy *The Broken Heart*, I. 3, Orgilus, disguised as a scholar, occupies the stage when his sister Euphranea and her lover Prophilus enter. Orgilus, pretending to be deep in his book, steps aside and listens to the couple, who on their part are supposed to be unaware of a third person's presence. The lines are divided as follows:

Orgilus (*aside*):   . . . my mind is busy,
 Mine eyes and ears are open.
Proph. (*to Euphranea*):   Do not waste
 The span of this stolen time, lent by the gods . . .

Prophilus is supposed not to have heard what Orgilus said; and yet he starts his own speech exactly where Orgilus has broken off, thus continuing the five-foot iambus.

A few lines farther down we find the following passage:

Proph.:   . . . a friend
 Firm and unalterable.
Org.: (*aside*):   But a brother
 More cruel than the grave.
Euphr. (*to Proph.*):   What can you look for
 In answer to your noble protestations . . .

It is quite in order for Orgilus to continue the line started by Prophilus; for Orgilus is eavesdropping and is expected to hear what Prophilus says. It is, however, strange that Euphranea should continue Orgilus's line. According to the stage-convention she has "not heard" what Orgilus said. We should, therefore, assume that she would either continue her lover's verse with whom she is talking, or start a line of her own. Yet she continues the verse started by Orgilus.

And thus it goes on. In that single scene the hidden Orgilus breaks into the couple's dialogue nine times, but in no case is the regular flow of the verse interrupted. What are the two lovers expected to do while Orgilus has his short soliloquies? Each time they have to stop talking, to listen without appearing to be listening, and only then to resume their conversation. How forced! how against the stage! But that is Ford's method of dealing with that problem; he put the regularity of versification higher than anything else.

Ben Jonson follows the same principle. In *Sejanus*, III. I, Arruntius has several "asides", but the versification is never broken. (In the Folio 1616 the "asides" are put between brackets, to make sure that they are recognized as such.)

Tiberius: But, if the senate still commands me serve,
   I must be glad to practise my obedience.
Arr. (*aside*):
   (You must, and will, sir. We do know it.)
Senators: Caesar,
   Live long, and happy, great, and royal Caesar;
   The gods preserve thee, and thy modesty,
   Thy wisdom, and thy innocence!
Arr. (*aside*):   (Where is't?
   The prayer's made before the subject.)
Senators: Guard
   His meekness, Jove. . . .

Again, how unnatural and against the stage! The Senators make a pause for Arruntius to speak and then, although they "have not heard" a word of his speech, continue where he stopped, providing most submissively even the fifth foot:

Guard
His meekness, Jove, his piety, his care. . . .

It is obvious that Ben Jonson, when writing his verse, thought less of the actor than of the reader, less of the stage than of the book—in fact, that he was more anxious to be a poet than a playwright.

Another passage from Ben Jonson: in *The Fox*, IV. I, Sir Politick Would-be and Peregrine have the following lines:

Sir P.:   . . . with certain projects that I have;
       Which I may not discover.
Pereg. (*aside*):   If I had
       But one to wager with, I would lay odds now,
       He tells me instantly.
Sir P.:   One is, and that
       I care not greatly who knows, to serve the state
       Of Venice with red herrings for three years. . . .

Peregrine's is a genuine "aside": Sir Politick is "not to hear" his remark; and yet he continues the broken-off line to perfection.

Beaumont and Fletcher, *The Maid's Tragedy*, IV. 2:

Melanthius: But 'tis the king, the king, the king, Amintor,
       With whom thou fightest. (*Aside*) I know
               he's honest,
       And this will work with him.
Amintor: I cannot tell
       What thou hast said; but thou hast charm'd
               my sword. . . .

How does Shakespeare handle an "aside"? Is he in the same way as Ben Jonson and the others more interested in the uninterrupted flow of verse than in the logical demands of the stage? Is he, too, more concerned with prosody than stagecraft?

(1)

In *King Lear*, I. I. 77 ff., Regan finishes her speech of flattery; the subsequent lines are divided like this:

> And find I am alone felicitate
> In your dear highness' love.
>
> Cord: Then poor Cordelia,
> And yet not so, since I am sure my love's
> More ponderous than my tongue.
>
> Lear: To thee, and thine hereditary ever,
> Remain this ample third. . . .

Cordelia was listening to Regan and, therefore, continues her sister's verse. Lear on the other hand is supposed not to have heard what Cordelia said, and so starts a new line. That Cordelia, by leaving her last line short, tears a gap in the texture of the versification does not bother Shakespeare: his aim is not primarily to write verse but drama. Ben Jonson would have written something like this:

>   my love's
> More ponderous than my tongue.
>
> Lear: This ample third
> Remain to Regan and her house for ever. . . .

That, no doubt, would have been "regular" versification. But then, how could we know that Cordelia's lines are an "aside"? Shakespeare himself did not insert the word "aside", yet the text shows plainly enough two facts: (a) that Lear fills in the pause between his listening to Regan and his next speech by turning to the map: otherwise he could not speak of "*this* ample third"; and (b) that he has been unaware of Cordelia's words: otherwise he would not start a line of his own.

With Shakespeare, therefore, in contrast to Jonson's and the others' practice, it seems to be the rule that a character starts or resumes his speech with a new line, if he speaks on his own initiative· and that he continues a line broken off by another speaker only by way of replying to him.

This little rule has still to be confirmed; should it bear examination it might become the point from which to set forth in search for other features of Shakespeare's diction.

(2)

King Lear, v. 3. 96 ff.:

> Than I have here proclaim'd thee.
> Reg.:   Sick, O, sick!
> Gon. (*aside*): If not, I'll ne'er trust medicine.
> Edm.: There's my exchange: what in the world he is. . . .

Goneril's line is a soliloquy. The next speaker, Edmund, is not supposed to have heard it; he, therefore, starts a new line.

(3)

Hamlet, III. I. 43 ff.: Polonius arranges the scene for the great soliloquy by bidding Ophelia read her book, etc. The King has an "aside" which concludes with the lines:

> Than is my deed to my most painted word.
> O heavy burden!
> Pol.:   I hear him coming, let's withdraw, my lord.

It is clear that Polonius, looking out for Hamlet, was not listening; nor was he supposed to listen to the King's self-revelation: otherwise he would not—he of all persons! —start a new line.

It sometimes happens that on one side of the stage some conversation is going on that to those on the other side is tantamount to an "aside". In such a case the same rule applies, namely that the next speaker, irrespective of a broken-off line, starts a new one.

(4)

Hamlet, v. 2. 272 ff.:

Haml.:   Your skill shall like a star i'th' darkest night
          Stick fiery off indeed.
Laert.:   You mock me, sir.
Haml.: No, by this hand.
King: Give them the foils, young Osrick. Cousin
                              Hamlet. . . .

What Hamlet and Laertes say to each other is, so to speak, a private talk; the King does not take part in it: he has to start a line of his own.

He does the same a few lines later:

Haml.: This likes me well. These foils have all a length?
Osr.:   Ay, my good lord.
King: Set me the stoops of wine upon that table. . . .

II

ENTRIES

DOES it ever happen that on entering the stage a person begins his speech in the middle of a line? Not with Shakespeare, one would say; but with others this can be found over and over again. Those writers show a veritable "horror vacui" that compels them to avoid all breaks in versification. In their writings unfinished lines must be completed at any cost, any gap that happens to come about must be filled in—be it even by making a new character continue a line of which he has not "heard" a word.

John Ford, *The Broken Heart*, II. 2:
Armostes: The princess, with your sister.
          Enter Calantha—and others.
Calantha: I present you
          A stranger here in court, my lord; for did
                                        not . . .

At the end of the same scene:
Bassanes: I will be fell, and fell.
          Re-enter Groneas.
Groneas: My lord, you are called for.
Bassanes: Most heartily I thank you: where's my wife,
                                        pray?

The same play, IV. 2:
Bassanes: The calms of my composure.
          Enter Orgilus.
Orgilus: I have found thee,
          Thou patron of more horrors than the bulk. . . .

John Webster, *The Duchess of Malfi*, I. 1:
Cardinal: He comes: I'll leave you.
          Exit.—Re-enter Bosola.

Bosola: I was lur'd to you.
Ferdinand: My brother, here, the cardinal could never . . .

The same play, III, 1:
Antonio: They dream of.
Delio: The lord Ferdinand
            Is going to bed.
             Enter Ferdinand—and others.
Ferdinand: I'll instantly to bed,
            For I am weary. I am to bespeak. . . .

Philip Massinger, *The Roman Actor*, II. 1:
Parthenius: To make my father know what cruelty
            He uses on himself.
            Enter Paris.
Paris: Sir, with your pardon
            I make bold to enquire the emperor's pleasure.

John Fletcher, *The Faithful Shepherdess*, I. 3:
Cloe: Makes me complain.
            Enter Thenot.
Thenot: Was ever man but I
            Thus truly taken with uncertainty. . . .

The same play, v. 3:
Priest: Retire a while
            Behind this bush, till we have known that vile
            Abuser of young maidens.
            They retire. Enter Sullen Shepherd.
Sull. Sheph.:   Stay thy pace,
            Most loved Amarillis; let the chase . . .

Beaumont and Fletcher, *Philaster*, IV. 3:
Phil.:   Queens ought to tear their hair, and with
                         their tears
            Bathe them. Forgive me, thou that art the
                              wealth
            Of poor Philaster.

Enter King.

King: Is the villain ta'en?

Ben Jonson, *Sejanus*, II. I:

Eudemus: To take acquaintance of them.
               Re-enter Sejanus.

Sejanus: I must make
            A rude departure, lady: Cæsar sends . . .

Every Man Out of His Humour, II. 2:

Macil.:   This have I done, and this I think will please
                                              her.

            Behold, she comes.
               Enter Fallace.

Fall.:   Here's a sweet stink indeed!
            What, shall I ever be thus crost and plagued. . .

The Fox, V. I:

Mosca: Two suits of bedding, tissue—
Voltore: Where's the will?
            Let me read that the while.
               Enter Servants, with Corbaccio in a chair.

Corbaccio: So, set me down,
            And get you home.
Voltore: Is he come now, to trouble us!

Now, from Ford, Webster, Massinger, Fletcher, Beaumont, and Jonson, let us turn to Shakespeare: how does he deal with that problem?

First, however, I have to explain one aspect of my procedure. It will be seen that throughout my enquiry I have confined myself to examining those plays that are certain to be Shakespeare's own. If you wish to find out Rubens's peculiar technique you must examine those of his pictures only that have not been touched up by others. You must be sure that there is no collaboration such as in some pictures that are euphemistically called "School of

Rubens". Without that precaution you are bound to get foreign admixtures into the material from which you want to draw your deductions. In order, therefore, to avoid any possibility of falsification I have restricted myself to scrutinizing those of the plays that are indisputably free from any aspersion of collaboration.

By leaving aside the other plays I feel I have not lost anything; on the contrary it seems to me that the results of my research may be deemed to be all the more reliable. Where after all can a master be expected to show his technique if not in his universally acknowledged masterpieces? I think it is a safe assumption that Shakespeare's technique of versification, etc., can confidently be deduced from his great tragedies and those of the comedies that are his beyond doubt. The technical devices we find there can certainly be used as proofs or otherwise of Shakespearianity—if such a word is permitted.

The problem is this: A character on the stage finishes speaking, but the speech itself ends with an incomplete line. Another character now enters. Does he or does he not continue the metrical line left unfinished by the last speaker? In each of the examples just considered we saw that the newcomer does indeed continue the line. What is Shakespeare's usage?

King Lear, I. 2. 22 ff.:

Edm.: Now, gods, stand up for bastards!
            Enter Gloster.
Glo.:   Kent banish'd thus! and France in choler parted!

The same play I. 4. 317 ff.:

Gon.:   That dotage gives it.
            Re-enter Lear.
Lear: What! fifty of my followers at a clap. . . .

The same play, II. 1. 87 ff.:

Glo.:   To make thee capable.

22

Enter Cornwall—and others.

Corn.: How now, my noble friend! since I came hither. . . .

Hamlet, III. 3. 71:

King: All may be well.
>*Enter Hamlet.*

Ham.: Now might I do it pat, now he is praying. . . .

The same play, IV. 2. 4 ff.:

Ham.: O, here they come.
>*Enter Rosencrantz and Guildenstern.*

Ros.: What have you done, my lord, with the dead body?

Macbeth, II. 3. 93 ff.:

Ban.: And say it is not so.
>*Re-enter Macbeth.*

Macb.: Had I but died an hour before this chance. . . .

The same scene, 103 ff.:

Macb.: Is left this vault to brag of.
>*Enter Malcolm and Donalbain.*

Don.: What is amiss?
Macb.:　　　　　　　You are, and do not know 't.

Othello, II. 1. 42 ff.:

3. Gent.: Of more arrivance.
>*Enter Cassio.*

Cassio: Thanks, you the valiant of this war-like isle.

Julius Cæsar, II. 1. 32 ff.:

Brutus: And kill him in the shell.
>*Re-enter Lucius.*

Lucius: The taper burneth in your closet, sir.

Measure for Measure, IV. 2. 109 ff.:

Duke: We shall proceed with Angelo.
>*Re-enter Provost.*

Prov.: Here is the head; I'll carry it myself.

The same play, v. i. 18 ff.:

Duke: And good supporters are you.
        Enter Peter and Isabella.
Peter: Now is your time, speak loud and kneel before him.

Shakespeare, it is seen, differs from his fellow-play-wrights. In his earlier plays (in *A Midsummer-Night's Dream* and others) he had been aiming at tidy versifica-tion; this he had achieved by bringing almost all the lines to their proper five-foot length. Thus no gaps were left and the problem of filling them in did not arise. Now, however, in the great plays he has ceased being a slave of prosody; he does not care any longer about uninterruptedness of his iambics. He breaks a line off when it suits him, and if there is a gap, that does not prevent him from letting the new character start a new line.

That, after all, is demanded by the logic of the stage. A player, just entering, is not supposed to have listened to the words that are his cue (just as little as he is sup-posed to hear an "aside"); he cannot, therefore, be expected to continue the metre. And Shakespeare, in contrast to Jonson and the others, is more concerned with the demands of the stage than of prosody: it is for the actor he writes, not for the reader.

III

PAUSES

THERE is yet another kind of gap in versification, caused neither by an "aside" nor by a character's entering. One example has been referred to in the Foreword: the passage from *Twelfth-Night*, I. 2. 43 ff.:

(1)

Viola and the Captain discuss Orsino, Olivia's refusal to be married, etc. Each takes up the line where broken off by the other: the sign of normal conversation. Suddenly there is a gap.

Cap.: Because she will admit no kind of suit,
    No, not the duke's.
Vio.: There is a fair behaviour in thee, captain;
    And though that nature with a beauteous wall
    Doth oft close-in pollution, yet of thee
    I will believe thou hast a mind that suits
    With this thy fair and outward character.
    I prithee—and I'll pay thee bounteously—
    Conceal me what I am. . . .

Why that break after "duke's"? Of course Shakespeare could have written something like this:

Cap.: No, not the duke's.
Vio.:   Thou show'st a fair behaviour;
    And though that nature with a beauteous wall . . .

Yet he did not write like that; he preferred to interrupt his verse. What was his reason?

The explanation seems to lie in the action. So far Viola

has not said anything about herself and her plans. Now, having extracted from the Captain the information she needed, the idea strikes her that sets the comedy in motion: her disguise as a boy. But the Captain knows her to be a girl. What is to be done? She must buy or bribe him—"bounteously", as she says later on—: but is he to be trusted? That is an important question; if he gives her away, her whole scheme would be spoiled. Scrutinizing his face she comes to the conclusion:

> There is a fair behaviour in thee, captain. . . .

and she believes:

> thou hast a mind that suits
> With this thy fair and outward character.

To come to this conclusion, however, she needs a few moments, be they ever so short. She will perhaps walk a few steps aside, think hard for a second or two, turn back and look into the Captain's face, and only then go on speaking. The brainwave about her disguise; the examination of the man's features; her decision: all that is packed into the short pause after "No, not the duke's."

(2)

Macbeth—in IV. I. 142 ff.—is told that

> Macduff is fled to England.

Macb..   Fled to England?
Lenn.: Ay, my good lord.
Macb.: Time, thou anticipat'st my dread exploits;
    The flighty purpose. . . .

Macduff's escape to England is the turning-point of the play: with it the revenge sets in. The news comes down on Macbeth as a mighty blow; he winces under it. That

is the meaning of the gap after "Ay, my good lord".
Macbeth needs a while to regain his balance: only then
he goes on:

Time, thou anticipat'st my dread exploits. . . .

(3)

In the last scene—v. 7. 40 ff.—Macbeth meets his end.
So far he has still been sure that no human being can slay
him. And now at last Macduff is facing him. Once more
he boasts of his own invulnerability:

I bear a charmèd life, which must not yield
To one of woman born.
Macd.:   ' Despair thy charm,
And let the angel whom thou still hast serv'd
Tell thee, Macduff was from his mother's womb
Untimely ripp'd.
Macb.: Accursèd be that tongue that tells me so;
For it has cow'd my better part of man. . . .

They use their words as though they were pointed
weapons. The points, deadly sharpened, are "of woman
born" and "untimely ripp'd": they are deliberately put
at the end of the sentences, intended to come down on
the opponent's head as crushing blows. But there is a
marked difference in their replies: after "of woman born"
Macduff continues the verse; after "untimely ripp'd"
there is a gap. May we assume, then, that the difference
in the way they reply is caused by a difference in their
reactions?

The first blow, dealt by Macbeth, fails. Macduff knows
how he was born: instead of being dismayed he replies in
triumph—and replies at once. Accordingly the line,
divided between them, remains unbroken. His riposte,

however, has a deadly effect: after "untimely ripp'd"
there is an ominous pause. So there is a man, not born
of woman! Macbeth recognizes that his end has come.
His last illusion has been destroyed. His charm is gone.
Suddenly confronted with death he staggers back and
sinks his sword. Only after a pause, full of that fatal
recognition, is he able to go on, now completely changed:

> Accursèd be that tongue that tells me so . . .
> . . . . I'll not fight with thee.

(4)

Othello, I. 3. 192 ff.: Brabantio realizes that he has lost
his daughter irrevocably; he renounces his rights as a
father:

> I had rather to adopt a child than get it.
> Come hither, Moor:
> I here do give thee that with all my heart
> Which, but thou hast already, with all my heart
> I would keep from thee.

It is obvious that the gap after "Come hither, Moor" is
made to allow Othello to come up to his unwilling father-
in-law.

(5)

In *Othello*, III. 3. 92 ff., we have the following pause:

Oth.: Excellent wretch! Perdition catch my soul
But I do love thee: and when I love thee not,
Chaos is come again.
Iago: My noble lord——
Oth.:   What dost thou say, Iago?

Othello gazes after Desdemona. Little does he know
that he is enjoying the last few moments of happiness in
his life and that Chaos personified stands only a few steps
away from him. In the pause after "Chaos is come again"
Iago slinks up to Othello and then, cautiously, pours the
first drop of poison into his master's ear: "My noble lord
. . . did Michael Cassio . . . know of your love?"

(6)

In *The Merchant of Venice*, iv. i. 109 ff., there is the
following gap:

Sol.:   My lord, here stays without
         A messenger with letters from the doctor,
         New come from Padua.
Duke: Bring us the letters; call the messenger.

There is a gap after "Padua". May we assume that
this gap, too, indicates a pause? The situation is this:
Bellario, the learned doctor, has not arrived; instead there
is a message from him. On hearing that, the Duke is
apparently obliged, if only by politeness, to find out
whether his fellow-judges, the Magnificoes, are agreed on
admitting the messenger; so he probably turns to the
right and left to see whether he has his colleagues' concurrence, and only after their nodded consent he pronounces the Court's decision:

Bring us the letters; call the messenger.

(7)

In the same scene—310 ff.—Portia has at last awarded
the pound of flesh. Shylock is overwhelmed with jubila-

tion: "Most rightful judge! . . . Most learnèd judge!"
But then comes the tail-piece of her sentence:

> if thou dost shed
> One drop of Christian blood, thy lands and goods
> Are by the laws of Venice confiscate
> Unto the state of Venice.

Graz.: O upright judge! Mark, Jew! O learnèd judge!

Is the gap after "state of Venice" deliberate? I think
it is; it indicates a pause of stupefaction. The hearers are
struck with amazement; they gaze at each other, not yet
grasping the fact that the danger has passed—until
Graziano, first in understanding the catharsis, breaks in
with his jeering, starting of course a new line.

It was the producer in Shakespeare who, while writing
the scene, foresaw the dramatic effect of that pause; but
(and that is what Jonson never thought of doing) instead
of demanding the pause in a foot-note or a stage-direction
or leaving it to the producer's discretion, he preferred to
make the pause himself: in the text.

(8)

In *Measure for Measure*, II. 2. 45 ff., Isabella, pleading
for her brother's life, loses hope and is about to retire.
Lucio persuades her to try once more:

> Give't not o'er so: to him again, entreat him
> . . . .
> You could not with more tame a tongue desire it:
> To him, I say.

Isab.: Must he needs die?
Ang.:   Maiden, no remedy.

The pause after "To him, I say" has been made to
allow Isabella to walk up towards Angelo.

(9)

Othello, in III. 3. 116 ff., asks Iago to reveal what he thinks.

Oth.:   if thou dost love me,
    Show me thy thought.
Iago: My lord, you know I love you—
Oth.:   I think thou dost
    And for I know thou'rt full of love and honesty . . .

Iago does not answer at once, or he would continue Othello's line. He pretends to hesitate, by which little play he means to whet his master's appetite. His words are not a plain and open assertion of friendship, but a cautious prologue to what he is going to tell his victim. They are intended to sound as though overshadowed by some threatening cloud. Iago will probably look aside uneasily, slowly shake his head or in other way demonstrate how much against his grain it is to speak at all, and only then will he say in a markedly hesitating manner:

    My lord, you know I love you—

(10)

Hamlet, IV. 7. 21 ff.:
Claudius has a lengthy conversation with Laertes, replying to his questions. In the end all objections are answered; Laertes appears to be satisfied.

                              so that my arrows . . .
    Would have reverted to my bow again,
    And not where I had aim'd them.
Laer.: And so have I a noble father lost,
    A sister driven into desperate terms. . . .

Laertes does not continue the King's last line, but

31

starts a new one. The reason seems to be that he discontinues the conversation: he does not reply, but sums up in his mind, almost soliloquizing, what he has been told. It is only after a pause of recapitulation that he gives that résumé of his bereavement.

Discontinued verse signifies discontinued conversation.

(11)

In *Twelfth-Night*, III. 4. 376 ff., Antonio, mistaking Viola for her brother, wants the money repaid which he imagines he had lent her. Viola, who had never before set eyes on Antonio, does not understand what he is talking about.

Ant.: I must entreat of you some of that money.
Vio.: What money, sir?
     For the fair kindness you have show'd me here. . . .

The gap after "sir" is unmistakably a pause of dumb action. Viola stares at her unknown rescuer, waiting for an answer, while he is speechless at what he cannot but regard as brazen-faced ingratitude. Only after that short pause of mutual amazement Viola, left without an answer, goes on with her speech.

(12)

King Lear, I. I. 169 ff.: Kent does his best to make his old master revoke that fateful decision. Lear rages; but Kent does not stop talking:

               Revoke thy gift,
Or whilst I can vent clamour from my throat
I'll tell thee thou dost evil.

Lear: Hear me, recreant,
        On thine allegiance, hear me!
        Since thou hast sought to make us break our
                                            vow. . . .

Kent's last words and Lear's "Hear me, recreant" form
one iambus: one speaker takes over from the other. The
next line, however, is broken off, and as a result we have
a pause.

From the producer's point of view the pause is not
merely obvious, but necessary. Having at last silenced
his vassal (which he achieves only by appealing to his
allegiance) Lear is now judge and prepares to pass
sentence: banishment or death. No judge would pronounce a sentence such as this without first making a
pause of complete silence. It is this pause that Lear makes
—or Shakespeare makes for him.

(13)

In *Othello*, I. 3. 60 ff., Brabantio accuses a man, whom
as yet he does not name, of having seduced his daughter,
which, he alleges, could not have been accomplished except
by sorcery.

        Being not deficient, blind, or lame of sense,
        Sans witchcraft could not.
Duke: Whoe'er he be that, in this foul proceeding,
        Hath thus beguil'd your daughter of herself. . . .

It would show improper haste in the Duke should he
reply instantly, without any pause of deliberation. It is
more dignified for him first to take in the full import
of the accusation before he pronounces the decision to
appoint Brabantio judge in his own case—which after all,

33

in the alleged case of black magic, is tantamount to a
sentence of death.

(14)

In *Macbeth*, I. 4. 24 ff., Duncan welcomes his victorious
generals. If we disregard the changes made by the editors,
but rely on the line-division of the Folio, the passage reads
like this:

> And our duties are to your throne and state
> Children and servants; which do but what they
> > should,
> By doing everything safe toward your love
> And honour.
>
> Dunc.:　　　　　Welcome hither:
> I have begun to plant thee, and will labour
> To make thee full of growing. Noble Banquo,
> That hast no less deserv'd, nor must be known
> No less to have done so: let me enfold thee
> And hold thee to my heart.

In the case of Banquo, Duncan not only embraces him
but expressly says so. But surely he does no less to
Macbeth, his first general (and cousin) whom he moreover
welcomes first? After "welcome hither" he embraces him
—and, to make room for that short action, there is the
gap in the metre.

Music does not consist of notes only, but of pauses also;
they are just as important as the notes. Jump the rests
in a composition, and what will become of it? Yet during
the rests the tension between the notes does not cease; on
the contrary, it may be strengthened by the short silence
in between. Rests in music and pauses in dramatic speech
have the same function.

34

But there is yet another group of pauses which, were I allowed to use a musical term, I should like to call "rests"; but the word "metrical gaps" will do as well.

Such rests and stops may be found everywhere in Shakespeare's later word-symphonies. How did he mark them? He marked them by making them.

IV

METRICAL GAPS

(I)

Othello, in III. 3. 380 ff., takes Iago by the throat. Iago, deeply "offended", turns away and makes for the exit. That he really puts a full stop to his connection with Othello—or at least wishes to give that impression—is shown by the rhyme with which he concludes his speech.

> O monstrous world! Take note, take note, O world!
> I thank you for this profit and from hence
> I'll love no friend, sith love breeds such offence.
> Oth.: Nay, stay: thou shoudst be honest.
> Iago: I should be wise; for honesty's a fool. . . .

Iago actually goes. Othello calls him back: "Nay, stay!" Iago stops, very much "against his will", and stands, a sullen picture of offended dignity. Othello comes up to him, perhaps turns him round to look into his face, or perhaps looks him up and down—and only after some such mute action will he go on to say, and certainly in a changed voice: "Thou shoudst be honest".

That there really is a pause between "Nay, stay" and "thou shoudst be honest" is indicated by the "deficiency" of the metre. The metre, however, is deficient only if we fail to see the gap and do not allow for that short moment of dumb acting. Moreover, the Folio text has a colon after "stay". This colon, however, has in the editions been changed into a semicolon—a change that does away with the pause completely.

(The first editor of the play, as I call him, i.e. the man who prepared and "corrected" the text for the Quarto of 1622, changed the colon into a comma, thus making things still worse. Apparently no actor, he misunderstood Shakespeare's punctuation as well as his theatrical subtleties. About that man more will have to be said later on.)

(2)

In *Macbeth*, I. 3. 88, Banquo is interrupted by the entry of Ross and Angus:

Toth' selfe-same tune, and words: who's here?
x — x — x — / (x —) x —

After "words" two syllables are missing. Their space and time is filled in by the pause in which Banquo turns to see who is coming.

(Hanmer thought it necessary to "complete" the line: he substituted "But who is here?" for "Who's here?")

(3)

Lady Macbeth (I. 5. 38 ff.) learns of the King's visit. After the messenger has gone she says:

> The raven himself is hoarse
> That croakes the fatal entrance of Duncan
> Under my battlements. Come, you spirits,
> That tend on mortal thoughts, unsex me here. . . .

The first sentence differs emotionally from the next. After "battlements" the Lady gathers her strength: what follows is a solemn invocation, calling upon the "murdering ministers". Whether the actress takes a step forward, or raises her arms, or looks round, or simply takes a deep breath: there will always be a small pause; the text itself demands it imperatively—and here the pause is, clearly shown by the gap in the metre: between "battlements" and "Come" one syllable is missing.

(And yet, one of the latest editors of the play—in *The*

Arden Shakespeare—holds that "nothing can account for the missing syllable"; to him, the line is "distinctly incomplete". He refers to Steevens's suggestion: "Come, come, you spirits . . ." and to Pope's: "Come, all you spirits". He himself, however, thinks that the reading "ill spirits" ought to be adopted. One wonders whether Shakespeare would be grateful for such collaboration.)

(4)

Hamlet, III. I. 66 ff.:

> For in that sleep of death, what dreams may come,
> When we have shuffled off this mortal coil,
> Must give us pause. There's the respect . . .

In the last line, which has four stresses only, Hamlet not only speaks of pausing, but actually makes a pause: between "pause" and "There's". The actor will not find it difficult to follow the author's advice. If only he thinks of what he just said (that the possibility of dreams after death makes us hesitate) and with a nod, or a slight turn of his head, pauses long enough as to think: "Alas!" or "Yea, so it is!", thus inserting, if only in thought, the missing syllables, and only then goes on: "There's the respect", he will find nothing "irregular" in the line.

(5)

Hamlet, II. I. 74 ff.: Ophelia enters, highly upset by Hamlet's visit.

Pol.: How now, Ophelia! what's the matter?
Oph.: Alas, my lord, I have been so affrighted—
Pol.: With what, in the name of Heaven?
Oph.: My lord, as I was sewing in my chamber . . .

To begin with, we have a short pause after "Heaven", indicated by a gap in verse. It is a pause of breathless agitation; Ophelia must regain her composure before she starts with her story.

The eight lines of her next speech are—in the Folio—pointed with commas only:

> My lord, as I was sewing in my chamber,
> Lord Hamlet with his doublet all unbrac'd,
> No hat upon his head, his stockings foul'd,
> Ungarter'd, and down-gyvèd to his ancle,
> Pale as his shirt, his knees knocking each other,
> And with a look so piteous in purport,
> As if he had been loosèd out of hell,
> To speak of horrors: he comes before me.

In the last line, after "horrors", one syllable seems to be missing; and so it is: but in its place there is a pause.

The eight lines are spoken hurriedly; that is shown by their punctuation: Ophelia speaks in a disturbed and disturbing way. When she finally arrives at "to speak of horrors" she stops for a moment, gulps down her agitation, and only then is she able to finish her sentence: "he comes before me".

(The editors, however, have not only changed five of the commas into semicolons, thus slowing down and spoiling the tempo, but, to make matters still worse, have eliminated from the last line the colon and put a comma instead, thus obliterating the pause that Shakespeare was so meticulous to insert.)

(6)

Othello, in II. 3. 217 ff., having put an end to the fight between Montano and Cassio, wishes to find the culprit.

> To manage private and domestic quarrel?
> In night, and on the court and guard of safety?
> 'Tis monstrous: Iago, who began't?

In the last line one syllable is missing. Are we to assume (as Abbott does in his *Shakespearian Grammar*) that the author wants us to pronounce "monst(e)rous"? It seems more plausible that Othello, after "monstrous", turns away from the two suspects and jerks his head toward Iago before he addresses him. To allow this turn there is the gap.

(And yet Capell, Steevens, and Keightley actually print: "monsterous", whereas Pope thought fit to cut the Gordian knot by the simple means of inserting the missing word; he reads and prints: "Say, Iago . . .".)

(7)

In *Macbeth*, I. 4. 11 ff., Duncan has been told of Cawdor's death, and remarks:

> there is no art
> To find the mind's construction in the face:
> He was a gentleman, on whom I built
> An absolute trust.
> > *Enter Macbeth, Banquo, Rosse, and Angus.*
> > O worthiest cousin,
> The sin of my ingratitude even now . . .

In this passage Shakespeare apparently does not wish to have any longer pause caused by Macbeth's entry; or he would after "absolute trust" have broken off the line and let Duncan start a new one. The fact that the words: "O worthiest cousin" continue the line is I think an indication that Macbeth and the others have entered behind him, with the result that Duncan does not need more than to turn round, or simply turn his head—to look into his murderer's face. The turn itself, away from Malcolm and towards Macbeth, is indicated by the little gap between the two parts of the line.

Why does Shakespeare, the producer, take care, as he evidently does, not to have a longer pause just there? It is probably because he wishes to stress the suddenness with which Macbeth occupies the place of the traitorous Cawdor. One moment Duncan says that there is no trusting anybody's face; the next moment, beaming with joy and ill-placed gratitude, he trusts him who is planning his death. The quicker the transition from no-trust to full-trust, the quicker the replacement of the dead traitor by the living murderer, the more impressive it is.

(8)

In Part I, *King Henry IV*, v. 4. 68 ff., Percy, slain by Prince Henry, is dying. The passage reads in the Folio like this:

> No Percy, thou art dust
> And food for——
> *Prin.:* For Wormes, braue Percy. Farewell great heart:

Percy is forced to break off; interrupted by the "fell sergeant, death". During the long pause, as indicated by the gap, Percy breathes his last gasp. The Prince finishes the broken-off sentence: "—for worms, brave Percy.". Then, either sinking his sword or making some other gesture of reverence, he bids his noble foe farewell: "Farewell, great heart". It seems to be in keeping with Shakespeare's diction that before these words, in order to allow for that short gesture, there should be a small pause—and there it is: one syllable is missing.

(The editors, however, thought it their duty to regularize what they regarded as a "faulty line": silently they inserted the missing syllable, and thus it is that in all modern editions the words: "Farewell, great heart" have been exchanged for: "Fare thee well, great heart".)*

(9)

Othello, in I. 3, at the end of the "hair-breadth 'scapes", the Anthropophagi, etc., comes to the line 144:

> and men whose heads
> Grew beneath their shoulders. These things to
> hear . . .
>
> x (x) — x — x (—) x — x —

After "shoulders" there is a gap: one syllable missing. Othello has finished one chapter of his story: adventures abroad; now he turns to another subject: to Desdemona. It should be natural for him to stop for a moment: he might take a deep breath or change his attitude or whatever the actor might find to fill in that gap that comes of itself when, so to speak, one turns over to the next page.

And Shakespeare has actually made the pause. The editors, however, seeing the irregularity of the metre, consulted the Quarto 1622—and there they found the line "corrected" like this:

> Do grow beneath their shoulders. This to hear . . .

Of course they preferred this to the Folio reading and, accordingly, that has become the generally accepted text. Yet after so many parallel instances quoted, it seems to me to be obvious that it was a man unfamiliar with Shakespeare's peculiarities of diction who "regularized" this and so many other lines in his Quarto edition—which, although published one year before the Folio, appears to be a touched-up version of the original text as preserved in the Folio.

* Also in the *Cambridge* edition, edited by Professor J. Dover Wilson.

(10)

Macbeth, IV. 3. 109 ff.: Macduff, after his long conversation with Malcolm, despairs of this future king of Scotland.

> The Queen that bore thee,
> Oftner upon her knees than on her feet,
> Died every day she liv'd. Fare thee well.

As in the other examples there is, in the last line, a short gap. Macduff is at the end of his tether; he gives up all the hopes with which he had come. How he puts that full stop to his endeavours, by raising an arm and dropping it in despair, or stepping back, or merely by taking a deep breath, must be left to the actor. Yet some such indication of finality Shakespeare must have wished for, or he would not have marked that pause.

(The editor of the play in *The Arden Shakespeare*, however, maintains that, unless we are to accentuate the termination of "lived", the line must be regarded as faulty in metre. He suggests that either an "O" has been left out by the compositor—"O, fare thee well"—or that, as he prefers to think, the missing word is "then"—"Then fare thee well".)*

(11)

In *Macbeth*, I. 2. 40 ff., the Bleeding Sergeant comes to the end of his report. If we retain the line-division of the Folio, from which to deviate I cannot see any reason, his words read as follows:

> Except they meant to bathe in reeking wounds,
> Or memorize another Golgotha,
> I cannot tell: but I am faint,
> My gashes cry for help.

* Professor Dover Wilson, in the *Cambridge* edition, prints "livéd"; but the Folio has expressly "liu'd".

Dunc.: So well thy words become thee as thy wounds,
     They smack of honour both: Go get him surgeons.

After "I cannot tell" there is a gap of two syllables.
The man is completely exhausted. Either he takes a deep
breath or staggers back or shows in any other way that
he is on the point of fainting.

After "My gashes cry for help" there is a pause, one
of the type that has been dealt with in Chapter III. The
Sergeant threatens to break down, others probably rush
in to support him, or he would fall—and only after that
pause, filled in by action, the King, starting a new line,
pays him his tribute:

So well thy words become thee as thy wounds. . . .

(12)

In II. 2. 14 ff., Lady Macbeth has the following lines,
quoted with the verse-division and the punctuation of
the Folio:

         I laid their daggers ready,
He could not miss 'em. Had he not resembled
My father as he slept, I had done't.
My husband?

Between "as he slept" and "I had done't" there is a
gap of one syllable and, to make the gap more marked,
a comma is inserted. Whether after "slept" the Lady
throws back her head or makes a gesture with her hand
or takes a step forward, must be left to the actress. What,
however, the author-producer wants her to do definitely
is that she should stress the "I", which, if stressed, stands
for "I myself". In order to do so she must make a pause
before it—and there the pause is: in the text itself and,
in addition, indicated by the comma.

All the editors, however, interfere with the line-
division; they print:

My father as he slept, I had done't. My husband!
x — x — x — x x — x — x

—thus forcing the actress to stress not the "I" but the "done't", which is contrary to what Shakespeare wanted. (Some of them even omit the comma.) But surely it is not the same whether the Lady says: "I had *done* it" or: "I *myself* had done it"? The line should be scanned:

My father as he slept, I had done't.
x — x — x — (x) — x —

(13)

The following are the first lines spoken by Lady Macbeth when she enters (II. 2.):

That which hath made the[m] drunk, hath made
me bold:
What hath quench'd them, hath giuen me fire.

She contrasts "them—drunk" with "me—bold"; "quenched—them" with "given me—fire". That is expressed not merely in the words, but in the rhythm also. Yet since Rowe all editors print the second line as:

What hath quench'd them hath given me fire.
Hark! Peace!
x — x — x — x — x —

In this arrangement not only "quenched" loses its stress, the actress is also induced to pronounce "me" as unaccented; thus the scales of the comparison become unbalanced. I think the rhythm of the line is this:

What hath quench'd them, hath given me fire
x x — — / x — x — —

★

Before leaving the matter of pauses and gaps I should

45

like to say this. I do not assert that every gap in metre or every other irregularity in versification must have a theatrical meaning. Some of those irregular features are certainly due to shortcomings on the compositor's part; others may have been caused by negligence in the theatrical scribe (probably identical with the prompter) who wrote out the prompt-book; or by ignorance in a transcriber who (as, to my mind, in the case of the Quarto 2 of *Hamlet*) prepared the copy for the compositor; or, lastly, by indifference in the author himself.

This author, after all, was not so petty as to stick to any rules, not even to his own. We may be sure that those features of diction behind which we try to find rules were never worked out by him as a system, but that he invented and used them as he went, rather impulsively. He, unlike Ben Jonson, did little to gain the laurels of immortality. He did not write for book and posterity, but for the next production. No wonder, then, that he did not set great store by the demands of poetic polish or by the unruffled flow of tidily finished lines.

In these circumstances it may well be that many of those irregularities have come about by mere chance, without any special purpose attached to them. Nevertheless, the instances examined so far seem to show that it is worth while, wherever a pause or gap occurs, to try to find out whether it can be traced back to a theatrical or histrionic idea on the part of that eminent actor-producer.

V

IRREGULAR STRESSES

A CERTAIN type of verse appears so often and with such
obvious significance that it, too, must be reckoned among
the hall-marks of Shakespeare's diction.

In Lady Macbeth's line:

> My father as he slept, I had done't
> x — x — x — (x) — x —

it was apparently the author's wish that the actress,
before stressing the "I", should pause for a moment; in
order to make her do so he omitted the syllable before "I".

In the following instances similar pauses are intended.
In these cases, however, no syllable is missing, yet the
same result is achieved: by dint of shifting the stress.

One example has been given in the Foreword:

> The grey-ey'd morn smiles on the frowning night
> x — x — / — x x — x —

Lines of similar structure are to be found everywhere,
even in the Sonnets:

> Richer than wealth, prouder than garments' cost
>
> (91, 10)
>
> — x x — / — x x — x —

or:

> Happy to have thy love, happy to die (92, 12)
> — x x — x — / — x x —

That irregularity, it is obvious, is used to emphasize
the emotional freight of the line. And yet, to say that
is not enough. In the following instances, which are a
small selection only, the abnormal stress—the short pause,
often indicated by a comma, with the subsequent dactyl

47

—gives the line a touch of finality, sounding as if a heavy decision had been reached.

Romeo and Juliet, III. 1. 126:
    This but begins the woe others must end
    — x x — x — / — x x —

Othello, v. 2. 266:
    Here is my journey's end, here is my butt
    — x x — x — / — x x —

King Lear, v. 3. 323:
    I have a journey, sir, shortly to go
    — x x — x — / — x x —

Troilus and Cressida, I. 2. 320:
    Nothing of that shall from mine eyes appeare.
    — x x — / — x x — x —   (*Exit.*)

Troilus and Cressida, IV. 4. 139:
    To our own selves bend we our needefull talke.
    x — x — / — x x — x —   (*Exeunt.*)

Troilus and Cressida, v. 7. 8:
    It is decreed, Hector the great must dye. (*Exit.*)
    x — x — / — x x - x —

Othello, v. 1. 37:
    And your vnblest Fate highes: Strumpet I come:
    x x — x — — / — x x —

Antony and Cleopatra, v. 2. 289:
    To excuse their after wrath. Husband, I come
    x (x) — x — x — / — x x —

Macbeth, I. 2. 69:
    What he hath lost, noble Macbeth hath won. (*Exit.*)
    x — x — / — x x — x —

Hamlet, II. 1. 100:
And to the last, bended their light on me.
— x x — / — x x — x —

Hamlet, III. 2. 424:
To giue them Seales, neuer my Soule consent.
x — x — / — x x — x —   (*Exit.*)

Hamlet, III. 3. 98:
Words without thoughts, neuer to Heauen go.
— x x — / — x x — x —   (*Exit.*)

It is significant that all these lines occur either at a turning-point (as the instance from *Romeo and Juliet*) or at a moment of summing up or actually at the end of a speech, as in the instances from *Hamlet*, *Macbeth*, and *Troilus and Cressida*.

Why does Shakespeare employ this particular type of metre? Why does he not write:

> Words without thoughts will ne'er to heaven go

or:

> To give them seals do not consent, my soul

—and so forth? Because, to quote his own words:

> The current that with gentle murmur glides,
> Thou know'st, being stopp'd, impatiently doth rage.

First, he wants to achieve stronger effects by letting the pressure of emotional urge go high and releasing it suddenly; secondly, he wishes the actor to make a small pause and to fill it in by a short gesture.

Gesture always precedes the word. First comes the emotional reaction, i.e. the gesture; only then comes the word. Many actors are unaware of that; not so Shakespeare—a fact clearly shown by those passages.

(1)

Hamlet prepares to see his mother. He is now, after the "Mouse-trap", in no doubt about her guilt, at least as far as her adultery is concerned. Now, he says, he could do "such bitter business as the day Would quake to look on". What is this "bitter business"? Matricide. The idea actually enters his mind, but is refused. Cruel he intends to be, but:

> How in my words soever she be shent,
> To give them seals, never my soul consent.

If the actor honours Shakespeare's wish as expressed (1) in the shape of the verse and (2) in the comma after "seals", he will sweep away the idea of "giving seals", i.e. of using his dagger against his mother, either with a jerk of his head or with a quick gesture of his hand or by taking a step back from that horrifying vision—and only then, with an emphatic stress on the next syllable, go on to say: "never, my soul, consent".

(2)

King Claudius's line:

> Words without thoughts, never to heaven go

is of the same nature, even as to the comma. Also the gesture will be of a similar kind. "Words without thoughts"—shaking his head, or a helpless sweep of his hand—"never to heaven go."

(The editors have dropped the commas after "seals" as well as "thoughts"—despite their significance as to rhythm no less than gesture.)

(3)

Macbeth, I. 5. 53: The Lady, in her invocation of the "murdering ministers", wishes for the "dunnest smoke of hell",

> That my keen knife see not the wound it makes . . . .
> — x x — / — x x — x —

The Lady's whole tragedy lies in this verse as if in a seed. She wishes to use the knife, but she cannot bear to see the wound. When by Macbeth's negligence she is forced to take the daggers back to the slaughtered King, she is so shaken by what she sees that the picture haunts her for the rest of her life. In her sleep-walking it is still before her eyes:

> Yet who would have thought the old man to have had so much blood in him!

This incongruousness of her will-power and her nerve, her intellect and her emotional insufficiency, brings down on her what she had asked for: "the dunnest smoke of hell" that drives her into sleep-walking and finally into suicide.

Shakespeare makes the two syllables "knife" and "see" clash; he obviously wishes the actress to pause for a moment before "see". If she visualizes vividly enough the knife she speaks of, she will fill in that little pause very easily either by turning her head away from, or by closing her eyes to, that horrid vision or by stepping back from it; only then will she continue: "see not the wound it makes".

It may well be that the vision of the blood-dripping dagger Shakespeare apparently had when he wrote that line was the source for Macbeth's vision:

> Is this a dagger which I see before me?

The Lady imagines the dagger, but closes her eyes to it;

she swallows the dagger, so to speak, and dies of it, first mentally, and then killing herself. Macbeth sees the dagger, boldly goes for it, but cannot catch it. There, as though in symbolical contrast, we have the whole difference between their characters.

(4)

Macbeth, IV. 3. 194: Rosse prepares Macduff for the most dreadful news:

> but I have words
> That would be howl'd out in the desert air. . . .
> x — x — / — x x — x —

The meeting of the two heavy words "howl'd——out" with their long-drawn deep vowels is not only telling of, but themselves sounding, misery and pain.

(5)

Of the same type is the line quoted above from *Hamlet*:

> And to the last, bended their light on me.

Here again both rhythm as well as comma (omitted by the editors) indicate the author's wish—in this case his wish that the word "last" should be long enough to bridge over that gap caused by the clash of the two stressed syllables. Thus, by the very sound of the word "last", he expresses how long—to the very last moment—Hamlet kept his eyes on Ophelia.

★

Are we to assume that all those subtleties of diction have come about inadvertently, by mere accident? Of course not. We have to recognize them as what they are: the evidence and manifestation of a unique actor.

But—the objection is sure to be raised—was not

Shakespeare rather a poor actor? Don't we know what the parts are he himself used to perform? Adam in *As You Like It* and the Ghost in *Hamlet.* He never aspired to play Richard III or Lear or Othello. How, then, can he be called a great actor?

If we deny him that name then we cannot possibly call Beethoven a great musician. True, he wrote that Violin Concerto, but he could never have played it himself. Nor can Schubert be called a great composer of songs since he was unable to sing any of them himself. Nor did Brahms play the clarinet—and so forth. Of course, all that is utter nonsense. And yet we may hear it repeated time and again that Shakespeare most certainly was a poor actor because he himself was unable to play his own concertos, to sing his own songs, to perform the part of Macbeth.

In reality, just as Beethoven was a greater musician than a score of orchestras of first-class performers put together, so Shakespeare was a greater actor than Burbadge and his entire company and legions and generations of players, all rolled into one. What actually prevented him from playing the leading parts: whether he lacked the psychological staying-power necessary to concentrate for two hours on a single part, or whether it was the state of his teeth, or whether he was scant of breath, we have no means of knowing. We know, however, that he had sufficient breath, inexhaustible glass-blower that he was, to blow into existence all those multifarious bowls and vessels, graceful chalices and ugly bottles, proud goblets and big-bellied demijohns, each of them different from the other in outline and shape, yet ready waiting to be filled by the actors with the wine—or water—of their own emotions.

Who, after all, is an actor? Perhaps we could say: somebody who has the faculty of filling his own heart with somebody else's emotions. The comedian's art is somewhat different: he contents himself with imitating

E

others by copying their outward appearance and behaviour—as a child does who, putting on father's hat
and coat, pretends to be the doctor. The actor's art,
consisting as it chiefly does in feeling another person's
emotions, is not confined to the stage. A composer of
songs has first to soak his heart with the poet's emotions
before he sits down to set his words to music. It is not
the gift of inventing fine melodies that makes the great
composer, but that gift of taking up, as it were, another
person's heart-beat. If the artist depicts a weeping woman
standing beneath a cross he will fail in his task, this task
being to arouse emotions in the onlookers. Only when he
has filled his own heart to overflowing with what a mother
must feel who stands helpless by her son while he slowly
dies on the cross, only then will he be able to put some
of her, the mother's, feelings into his performance—and
only then will his performance move his spectators, move
them in a way similar to that in which a great actor can
move his hearers. All that is acting. Common to all of
them, painters, composers, players, is the ability to re-
kindle long-lost emotions, using for that purpose the
medium of their own hearts.

What, then, are we to call a man who was able to create
in his breast the feelings of Romeo and Othello, of Cleopatra and Lady Macbeth—and of so many others? Who
was able not only to generate within himself all those
emotions, but to clothe them with the flesh and blood of
his—no, of their own—language? A poor actor, indeed!

It was as early as 1592 that Henry Chettle said of
Shakespeare, the player, that he was

exclent in the qualitie he professes.

That was certainly true, and has been true since, and will
be true for all days to come. His quality as an actor, that
consists in his faculty of exchanging hearts, is unique in
this world.

VI

SIMULTANEOUSNESS

When in *Hamlet*, III. 2. 189, the Player-Queen interrupts her husband:

King: For husband shalt thou—
Queen: Oh, confound the rest. . . .

she actually interrupts him, i.e. she stops him: he breaks off, and she continues the line.

There are cases, however, where one character does not succeed in interrupting the other—with the result that for a while the two speak simultaneously.

(1)

In *Othello*, I. 1. 100 ff., it is evident that Roderigo is unable to interrupt Brabantio, who is venting his rage on him:

Brab.: Upon malitious knavery dost thou come
        To start my quiet.
Rod.: Sir! Sir! Sir!
Brab.:   But thou must needs be sure . . .

Remembering that in the Folio a full stop often stands for a dash, and seeing that the two half-lines before and after the threefold "Sir!" form a complete line, we have to conclude that Shakespeare wishes Brabantio to speak uninterruptedly, while it is left to Roderigo to insert his expletives where and when he can. A modern author, to make his idea clear, would probably add a stage-direction:

Upon malitious knavery dost thou come
To start my quiet, but thou must needs be sure,
My spirit and my place have in them power
To make this bitter to thee.

Rod.: (having tried several times to interrupt him with
shouts of "Sir!", now)

Patience, good sir!

(2)

Richard III, I. 3. 135 ff.:

Glo.: Poor Clarence did forsake his father, Warwick,
Ay, and forswore himself—which Jesu pardon!—
Marg.: Which God revenge!
Glo.: —to fight on Edward's party for the crown. . . .

An interjection, unnoticed or at least unheeded by
Gloucester, who speaks without interruption.

(3)

Hamlet, III. 4. 103 ff.:

Haml.: Save me and hover o'er me with your wings,
You heavenly guards! What would you, gracious
figure?
Queen: Alas, he's mad!
Haml.: Do you not come your tardy son to chide. . . .

(4)

Othello, in III. 3. 265 ff., is raging against Iago:

Make me to see't; or, at the least, so prove it
That the probation bear no hinge nor loop
To hang a doubt on; or woe upon thy life!

Iago: My noble lord—
Oth.: If thou dost slander her and torture me,
      Never pray more; abandon all remorse. . . .

Othello goes on storming, not allowing Iago to interrupt him.

(5)

King Lear, v. 3. 288 ff.:

Kent: No, my good lord; I am the very man—
Lear: I'll see that straight.
Kent: That, from your first of difference and decay,
      Have follow'd your sad steps.
Lear: You are welcome hither.
Kent: Nor no man else; all's cheerless, dark, and deadly...

This is the arrangement as found in the modern editions. Yet what Kent tries to make clear to his old master is this:

> No, my good lord, I am the very man
> That from your first of difference and decay
> Have follow'd your sad steps, nor no man else. . . .

To put a full stop after "sad steps" renders "nor no man else" senseless.

Lear does not listen to Kent or does not grasp what he is told. He mumbles something; but there is no logical connection between his and Kent's words and, accordingly, no rhythmical connection either. The passage is in fact another instance of simultaneous speaking, and should be printed as such:

Kent: No, my good lord, I am the very man—
Lear: I'll see that straight . . .
Kent: —that from your first of difference and decay
      Have follow'd your sad steps—
Lear: You are welcome hither . . .
Kent: —nor no man else. . . .

57

(6)

King Lear, II. 4. 99 ff.: Gloucester tells his king that Regan and her husband do not wish to see him.

Lear: I'd speak with the Duke of Cornwall and his wife.
Glo.:   Well, my good lord, I have inform'd them so.
Lear: Inform'd them! Dost thou understand me, man—
Glo.:   Ay, my good lord.
Lear: The king would speak with Cornwall, the dear
                    father. . . .

The "Ay, my good lord" does not fit into the verse texture: it is meant to be an interjection only. It seems impossible to assume that Lear—in his state of extreme agitation—should pause, wait for a reply to his (merely rhetorical) question and only then continue in his rage.

★

The instances dealt with so far have been interjections. There are, however, occasions where two or more characters talk simultaneously for a considerable length of time. This of course cannot happen in normal dialogue, but only in cases of violent altercation.

(7)

Othello, II. 3. 164 ff.—according to the Folio—:

Iag.   The Towne will rise. Fie, fie Lieutenant,
        You'le be asham'd for euer.
          Enter Othello, and Attendants.
Oth.:   What is the matter heere?
Mon.: I bleed still, I am hurt to th'death. He dies.
Oth.:   Hold for your liues.
Iag.:   Hold hoa: Lieutenant, Sir Montano, Gentlemen:
        Haue you forgot all place of sense and dutie?
        Hold. The Generall speaks to you: hold for shame.

Oth.:   Why how now hoa? From whence ariseth this?
Are we turn'd Turkes? and to our selues do that
Which Heauen hath forbid the Ottamittes.
For Christian shame, put by this barbarous Brawle:
He that stirs next, to carue for his owne rage,
Holds his soule light: He dies vpon his Motion.
Silence that dreadfull Bell, it frights the Isle,
From her propriety. What is the matter, Masters?

Montano's: "He dies" apparently means: "He [Cassio] shall die!"—and with that he renews his attack. The pedant who edited the Quarto 1622 omitted the words "He dies" altogether; he forced the line into a pitiful crawl:

'Zounds I bleed still, I am hurt to the death.
x — x — x — x — x —

In the Quarto 1630 on the other hand the words "He dies" have been substituted by a stage-direction: "He faints."

Of the modern editors not one follows the Folio: they either leave out Montano's battle-cry (with the result of a line that will hardly scan) or they order him to faint, which makes the continuance of his fight with Cassio appear somewhat ghost-like.

All editions print Othello's first words as though they continued Iago's line:

You'll be asham'd for ever.
What is the matter here?

Were this the correct arrangement it would militate against my theory that a character on entering the stage starts a new line. Yet I cannot accept that arrangement as correct, but hold that Othello starts an iambic of his own:

What is the matter here?

and continues it with the words:

>   Hold—for your lives—!

On the other hand Iago does not break off his line:

>   You'll be asham'd for ever—

but uninterruptedly goes on to:

>   —hold—ho—!

In fact, my suggestion is that all three, Iago, Montano, and Othello speak (or rather shout) simultaneously.

In the following I give the three parts of the text as a modern writer might have written them.

Iag.:   The town will rise. Fie—fie, lieutenant,
       You'll be asham'd for ever—hold!—ho—!
       Lieutenant, Sir Montano, gentlemen—
       Have you forgot all place of sense and duty?
       Hold!—The general speaks to you—hold—for
                               shame—

Mon.: [simultaneous with Iago:]
       I bleed still—I am hurt to th' death—he dies!

Oth.: [who, with attendants, has entered after: "You'll
       be asham'd for ever", shouting simultaneously with
       Iago and Montano:]
       What is the matter here? Hold! for your lives!
       Why—how now—ho! From whence ariseth this?
       Are we turn'd Turks? and to ourselves do that
       Which heaven hath forbid the Ottomites?
       For Christian shame, put by this barbarous brawl!
       He that stirs next, to carve for his own rage,
       Holds his soul light: he dies upon his motion!
        [Here he has outdone the others; there is silence.
       except for the bell.]
       Silence that dreadful bell; it frights the isle
       From her propriety. What is the matter, masters?

The simultaneousness is shown in the first place by the text. Iago says: "The general speaks to you"—not: he "has spoken" or: "will speak to you". Othello asks: "From whence ariseth this?" and not "hath arisen", which shows that "this", the brawl, is still on, at least down to Othello's words: "put by this barbarous brawl".

The simultaneousness is also borne out by the fact that in both Iago's and Othello's speeches the versification is not broken off by the other's (or Montano's) lines. As shown above, Iago's words:

> You'll be asham'd for ever—hold—ho

(if only "hold" is held out long enough) and Othello's:

> What is the matter here? Hold, for your lives!

form the usual iambics. The interruption of versification, as it appears in print, is one to the eye only. Yet it seems to be clear why Shakespeare breaks the lines: dividing them he uses the two parts as though they were brackets. Thus he indicates what he wishes his characters to do: speak simultaneously. As it is not his wont to give stage-directions it is difficult to see how else he could have expressed his intention. In a highly ingenious way he makes line-division serve as stage-direction.

He was not content to write the speeches one after the other and to tell the actors afterwards: "Here you will shout together"; but so vividly did he see and hear all the details of the uproar while inventing it that he put down the different voices in a way not dissimilar to that of a composer who writes the score of a trio.

(8)

Another brawl occurs in *Hamlet*, in v. i. 284 ff., when Hamlet and Laertes, in Ophelia's grave, come to blows.

We should expect a similar situation to show similar means of expression.

First we have a short passage in which three characters, either simultaneously or almost so, intersperse their exclamations into Hamlet's speech. One feels tempted to have the lines printed like this:

(Simultaneously:)

Hamlet:	King:
I prithee, take thy fingers from my throat;	Pluck them asunder!
	Queen:
Sir, though I am not splenetive and rash,	Hamlet, Hamlet!
	Gentl.:
Yet have I in me something dangerous	Good my lord, be quiet!
Which let thy wiseness fear.	
Away thy hand!	

Somebody, either the "Gentleman" (Folio) or Horatio (Quarto) succeeds in parting the two antagonists: that is shown by the fact that Hamlet no longer addresses Laertes directly ("Away thy hand!") but now merely refers to him: "I will fight with him. . . ."

After his outbreak: "I lov'd Ophelia . . ." Hamlet once more turns threateningly towards Laertes: "What wilt thou do for her?" Here the King begins to speak to Laertes: "Oh, he is mad . . .". The Queen, too, addresses him: "For love of God, forbear him!", but she is unable to interrupt her husband, who does not heed her interjection. Printed in the same way as suggested above, the whole passage would read like this:

(Simultaneously:)

Hamlet:	King:
I prithee, take thy fingers from my throat;	Pluck them asunder!
	Queen:
Sir, though I am not splenetive and rash,	Hamlet, Hamlet!

Gentl.:

Yet have I something in me dangerous

Good my Lord, be quiet!

Which let thy wiseness fear.
Away thy hand!*

Why, I will fight with him upon this theme

Queen:

Until my eyelids will no longer wag—

O my son, what theme?

I lov'd Ophelia, forty thousand brothers

Could not, with all their quantity of love,

Make up my sum. What wilt thou do for her?

King:

Come, show me what thou'lt do?

O, he is mad, Laertes—

Queen:

Woo't weep? woo't fight? woo't tear thyself?

For love of God, forbear him!

King:

Woo't drink up eisel? eat a crocodile?

—this is mere madness

I'll do't. Dost thou come here to whine?

And thus awhile the fit will work on him:

To outface me with leaping in her grave?

Anon as patient as the female dove,

Be buried quick with her, and so will I,

When that her golden couplet are disclos'd,

And if thou prate of mountains, let them throw

His silence will sit drooping.

Millions of acres on us, till our ground,

Singeing his pate against the burning zone,

Make Ossa like a wart! Nay, an thou'lt mouth,

* Quarto 2 has: "hold off thy hand,"—with a comma.

63

I'll rant as well as thou—
   Hear you, sir.
What is the reason that you
   use me thus?
I lov'd you ever; but it is no
   matter:
Let Hercules himself do
   what he may,
The cat will mew and dog
   will have his day. (*Exit.*)

Owing to his agitation Hamlet's speech runs off without any interruption. There is only one short pause, as shown by the gap in the metre, in the fifth line before the end:

     I'll rant as well as thou—Hear you, sir. . . .

This pause is obviously caused and taken up by (and made for) a gesture: Hamlet's mood is changing—as indicated also by the change·from "thou" to "you"—: he takes either a step or two towards Laertes or makes some other movement that may go with his attempt at reconciliation:

     What is the reason that you use me thus?
     I lov'd you ever—

Yet Laertes, drawing back or turning away, shows that he is not willing to be reconciled, and so Hamlet breaks off at once:

        —but it is no matter:
     Let Hercules himself. . . .

Examining the King's speech, we ought to remember from the passage in *Othello* that Shakespeare in a case such as this would be likely to break a line into halves in order to obtain what I have called "brackets". With the help of such brackets he would link together parts of a speech, thus indicating its uninterruptedness. In the present passage I take the brackets to be: "O, he is mad, Laertes" and "this is mere madness". Put together they seem to form a normal blank-verse:

O, he is mad, Laertes—this is mere madness. . . .

(The words "this is" are, as frequently in Shakespeare, to be pronounced as "this' mere madness"; in *Measure for Measure*, v. i. 132, we find: "This' a good Fryer belike", where the apostrophe after "This" indicates the absorption of "is".)

But, it might be objected, is not the assumption of those "brackets" nothing but an assumption? Is not the sentence: "O, he is mad, Laertes" complete in itself? Looking into the Folio, however, we find that after "Laertes" there is not, as we should expect, a full stop, but a comma:

Oh he is mad Laertes,

—a punctuation that, in this case, seems to have its significance.

Additional evidence appears to be provided by the First Quarto. There the equivalent of Hamlet's lines from: "I prithee, take thy fingers from my throat" until: "Make Ossa like a wart" is printed as one uninterrupted speech. On the other hand the equivalent for the King's: "O, he is mad, Laertes" and "This is mere madness" etc. is also printed as one unity. The whole passage reads in the Quarto like this:

I prethee take thy hand from off my throate,
For there is something in me dangerous,
Which let thy wisedome feare, holde off thy hand:
I lou'de Ofelia as deere as twenty brothers could:
Shew me what thou wilt doe for her:
Wilt fight, wilt fast, wilt pray,
Wilt drinke vp vessels, eate a crocadile? Ile doot:
Com'st thou here to whine?

> And where thou talk'st of burying thee a liue,
> Here let vs stand: and let them throw on vs,
> Whole hills of earth, till with the heighth therof,
> Make Oosel as a Wart.

King. Forbeare Leartes, now is hee mad, as is the sea,
Anone as milde and gentle as a Doue:
Therfore a while giue his wilde humour scope.

Ham. What is the reason sir that you wrong mee thus?
I neuer gaue you cause: but stand away,
A Cat will meaw, a Dog will haue a day.

Considering that this Quarto is evidently a pirate text, the passage appears to be well preserved. It is accurate even as to the exact spot where "thou" changes to "you". Moreover, it is only there (just where I pointed it out in my own arrangement) that Hamlet makes his first pause: before (in the Folio):

> Hear you, sir:
> What is the reason that you use me thus?

and before (in the Quarto):

> What is the reason sir that you wrong mee thus?

Down to this pause Hamlet's speech, printed in the Folio in four sections, appears in the Quarto as one uninterrupted passage. The King's speech, which in the Folio appears to be interrupted first by the Queen's interjection and then by Hamlet's challenge, shows in the Quarto no interruption at all. These points seem to support my suggestion of simultaneousness—especially if we keep in mind how, in all probability, the text of this "bad" Quarto has been achieved: it must have been made up either on the memory of one or two actors, or by stringing together paper strips containing the actors' parts.

The later Quartos (and, following them, all English editions as well as German translations, with the exception of my own) give the passage: "This is mere madness . . ." to the Queen. That, if correct, would do away with my assumption that this speech is a continuation of: "O, he is mad, Laertes". That the Folio is right, however, in attributing the speech to the King seems to be borne out by several circumstances:

(a) by the comma after: "O, he is mad, Laertes";

(b) by the stage-practice as shown in the First Quarto;

(c) by the two halves resulting, if put together, in one regular iambus; and

(d) by the words themselves, which seem to be more appropriate in the King's than the Queen's mouth. She would not, except in complete privacy (as in IV. I. 7), talk openly of Hamlet's madness; nor would she ridicule her own son by using that disparaging simile of the "female dove" with "her golden couplet". Such open mockery cannot be expected to come from the Queen.

Returning, however, to the question whether or not the passage can or ought to be regarded as one of simultaneous speech there must also, last but not least, be considered the situation on the stage. Should my suggestion be wrong, then we have to assume that Hamlet speaks his lines from: "Come, show me what thou'lt do" down to: "I'll rant as well as thou" as a solo, after which he has a long pause, and that into this pause the King puts in his own speech—an "aside" of four lines. Such an "aside" does not seem probable. Furthermore, Claudius tells Laertes, in order to assuage his wrath, that Hamlet's fit of madness "will work on him awhile" and that "anon" he will be silent. This announcement, if made when Hamlet has already ceased speaking, seems to be contradictory to the situation. If Claudius waits until Hamlet is silent his prediction that Hamlet "will be" silent is out of place. Equally, if he waits until Hamlet's rage has already subsided it makes no sense to say: "his fit will work on him awhile". The King's words are more in place if uttered before Hamlet stops, i.e. if they are spoken while he is still talking, or rather shouting.

But then, it might be objected, for a while neither Hamlet nor the King will be understood; their words will be drowned by each other. Yet is not this exactly what a good stage-producer would in any case try to achieve? An uproar on the stage, brought about by an ensemble of several voices (a usual thing in opera), is nothing extraordinary; the remarkable thing is only that Shakespeare did not leave the uproar to be produced during the rehearsals, but that he produced it even while he wrote it. He visualized and heard that tumult in advance: how Hamlet shouts at Laertes across the stage, how the royal couple take Laertes aside, and how all of them talk and exclaim at the same time. Does it matter whether or not their words can be understood? Not in the least. On the contrary, in the production of this scene (or that in *Othello*) the words themselves are of far less importance than their emotional contents. What ought to be shown —by using the words as mere voices as it were—is the general agitation, the tumultuous clash, even at the risk (which, if achieved, is a theatrical gain) of drowning in the hubbub the individual contributions to it.

Should my assumption of simultaneous speech be accepted, then the invention of those "brackets" and the "orchestral scoring", never employed by anyone else, would indeed be evidence of Shakespeare's consummate art as a stage-producer.

(9)

There is yet another instance of simultaneousness, in which, however, Shakespeare has expressed his intention less clearly. Although he divides a character's speech (to achieve "brackets") he does not go so far as to break off

68

single lines. This technique he apparently developed in his later plays only.

Romeo and Juliet, IV. 5. 33 ff.: the four, Father and Mother, Paris, and the Nurse—with Friar Laurence keeping in the background—stand around the bed on which, for all they know, Juliet lies dead.

Lady C.: Accurs'd, unhappy, wretched, hateful day

. . . .

Nurse: O woe, O woeful, woeful, woeful day

. . . .

Capul.: Despis'd, distressed, hated, martyr'd, kill'd

. . . .

Each of them has six lines; Paris alone seems to have four. Yet if the two lines he has prior to Lady Capulet are added to his later four, his text also amounts to six lines. Why have his lines been divided? I think for the same reason for which Shakespeare divided Iago's, Othello's, and Hamlet's lines—to use them as brackets.

In his book: *Shakespeare & The Popular Dramatic Tradition*, Mr. S. L. Bethell suggests that the scene should be understood and performed as burlesque. He finds the lamentations "ridiculous", and asserts that the audience is prompted to laugh at them. He maintains that "the tone of burlesque is clear enough" and that "only the astonishing ineptitude of Victorian criticism could have missed it."

Why the four mourners should behave in a "burlesque" way it is not easy to see. Actually they behave as the situation demands: they wail and, being Italians, they do so in an unrestrained manner. Weeping and wailing is infectious—and thus it is that what we hear is a four-part madrigal of wailing in which only the concerted sound is essential and not the meaning of the words.

It is true that the four "speeches" contain little more

than ejaculations, in particular the Nurse's lines. Dr. W. W. Greg, in his book *The Editorial Problem in Shakespeare*, goes even so far as to speak of "wholly un-Shakespearian verse". Yet those lamentations do not appeal to the intellect: they are merely inarticulate sounds of grief. The fact that the words as such are almost lost in the fourfold hubbub evidently accounts for their quality, which would be poor indeed if they were meant to be clearly understood.

That turmoil goes on until Friar Laurence interrupts it by shouting:

> Peace, ho! for shame! confusion's cure lives not
> In these confusions. Heaven and yourself . . .

What need should there be for the Friar to shout: "Peace, ho!" and "for shame!" had one speaker after another finished his or her speech in the ordinary way? It is obvious that his shout is necessary to bring to an end a violent uproar. Another indication is his expression: "These confusions"; it cannot mean the lamentations as such; what he means is their "confusedness"—their being uttered all at the same time.

Should evidence for my assumption still be needed it seems to be provided by a stage-direction, added in the First Quarto of the play; this direction reads:

> *All at once cry out and wring their hands.*

That "at once" has the meaning of "simultaneously" is borne out by the following two instances: *Macbeth*, I. 3. 44: ". . . each at once her choppy finger laying"—and *Much Ado About Nothing*, III. 2. 35: ". . . in the shape of two countries at once". (Also Milton, *Paradise Lost*, I. 788: "At once with joy and fear his heart rebounds.")

That stage-direction has hardly been penned by Shakespeare himself; but it must have been written down either by actors who had taken part in the performance and knew their business, or by pirates whose job it was to take away with them not only the text of the play but also as much as possible of the production and who, therefore, during the performance were using not only their ears but their eyes as well. In so far, that stage-direction, although of second-hand authority only, can be relied upon to express Shakespeare's own intention: that the four actors should "cry out at once", i.e. speak their parts simultaneously.

Shakespeare's stage practice, thus established in this case, certainly throws light also on the passages in *Hamlet* and *Othello*.

★

In *The Alchemist*, IV. 5, as printed in Ben Jonson's Folio of 1616, we find three characters on the stage: Dol, Face, and Mammon. Dol is "in her fit": she speaks incessantly, not allowing the others to interrupt her. First, to indicate the continuity of her talking, Jonson italicizes her speech and uses dashes. Later, however, he puts the stage-direction: "They speake together" and juxtaposes the two parts of the simultaneous passage. It looks like this:

. . . .

DOL. *To speake the tongue of* EBER, *and* IAVAN ——
MAM. O,
Sh'is in her fit. DOL. *We shall know nothing* —— FAC.
Death, sir,
Wee are vn-done. DOL. *Where, then, a learned Linguist Shall see the antient us'd communion Of vowels, and consonants* —— FAC. My master will heare!
DOL. *A wisedome, which* PYTHAGORAS *held most high* ——
MAM. Sweet honorable lady. DOL. *To compromise All sounds of voyces, in few markes of letters* ————

7¹

FAC. Nay, you must neuer hope to lay her now.

They speake together.

DOL. And so we may arriue by *Talmud* skill,
And profane *greeke*, to raise the building vp
Of HELENs house, against the *Ismaelite*,
King of *Thogarma*, and his *Habergions*
Brimstony, blew, and fiery; and the force
Of King ABADDON, and the Beast of *Cittim:*
With *Rabbi* DAVID KIMCHI, ONKELOS,
And ABEN-EZRA doe interpret *Rome.*

FAC. How did you put her into't?
MAM. Alas I talk'd
Of a fift *Monarchy* I would erect,
With the *Philosophers stone* (by chance) and shee
Fals on the other foure, straight.
FAC. Out of BROVGHTON!
I told you so. 'Slid stop her mouth. MAM. Is't best?
FAC. She'll neuer leaue. else. If the old man heare her,
We are but foeces, ashes. SVB. What's to doe there?
FAC. O we are lost. Now, she heares him, she is quiet.

Vpon Subtles entry they disperse.

The passage proves at least one thing: that simultaneous speech was not unknown on the Elizabethan stage—and we cannot assume that a theatrical device made use of by Ben Jonson should have been unfamiliar to Shakespeare.

The fact that nothing similar can be found in the Shakespeare Folio may be due to one or both of two reasons: that the pages of the Shakespeare Folio were halved (and half a page would have been too narrow for two texts to be printed side by side) and that Shakespeare as a writer was far less meticulous than Ben Jonson, who seems to have invented that trick of a two-column text.

VII

LINE-DIVISION

THE instances of incorrect line-division are very numerous. The editors did not always recognize the peculiar way in which Shakespeare treats his "asides". Only on rare occasions did they see any meaning in a pause or in a gap in verse. The possibility of simultaneous speech did not occur to them. Yet the main source of their interference with the line-division has been their misconception of what they regarded as Shakespeare's literary aspirations.

The editors, from Nicholas Rowe onward, were either scholars or scholarly poets. Common to all of them was the idea that Shakespeare was first and foremost a poet and that it is a poet's chief aim to write regular verse—such as they found in Ben Jonson's, John Ford's and others' writings and as Pope practised in his own work. Coming across a "faulty" line they seldom tried to find an explanation from the theatrical angle (still less did they think of any histrionic meaning) but either blamed the author's negligence, or the bad state of the manuscript, or they invented some mysterious collaborator, or finally, everything else having failed, it was the compositor's fault who did not know his job.

In his editors' opinion it was a great pity that so many mishaps concurred to obscure the purity of Shakespeare's genuine style and diction. Without those unfortunate accidents he would have left behind completely different texts, texts as perfect in versification and line-division as those by Ben Jonson or Pope himself. If only he had lived longer and been given the opportunity to make his lines tidy and read smoothly before the First Folio was set up, would he not have handed down to posterity a set

of plays free from all those textual blots? Since unfortunately, however, he was prevented from putting those
much-needed finishing touches to his work, it was for his
editors to see to it. To "regularize" the texts they considered their prime duty.

Such (admittedly exaggerated and put somewhat
crudely) was the attitude of those early editors. So far
very little has been done to correct their "corrections".
Almost all of the changes they have made have, alas!
been left untouched right down to our own day. Whichever edition one chooses, be it an ordinary or a scholarly
one, and wherever one opens the volume, one finds—
particularly in the great plays of the middle period—lines
re-arranged, punctuation altered, stage-directions inserted, etc.—all of which was substantially done in the
eighteenth century. Apart from the necessary business of
correcting the genuine misprints and apart from a handful
of emendations, most of those early alterations must be
said to be for the worse.

(1)

Measure for Measure, II. 2. 54 ff.: Isabella entreats
Angelo to pardon her brother. Lucio has come with her;
in his exuberant way he cannot hold his peace.

Isab.: If so your heart were touch'd with that remorse,
      As mine is to him?
Ang.:   He's sentenc'd, 'tis too late.
Luc.: You are too cold.
Isab.: Too late? Why, no; I, that do speak a word. . . .

The line-division is correct. Lucio does not take part
in the conversation; his words remain outside the dialogue
of the two chief characters and, therefore, outside the
verse texture. Accordingly Isabella does not take up

Lucio's line, but continues her dialogical connection with Angelo.

A different case, however, is the following passage (from the same scene, 108 ff.); it is usually printed like this:

Isab.:   . . . but it is tyrannous
       To use it like a giant.
Luc.:   That's well said.
Isab.: Could great men thunder
       As Jove himself does, Jove would ne'er be quiet. . . .

Does Lucio suddenly enter the conversation? Does he get an answer? No, he speaks "aside" or to himself. Nor does Isabella take any notice of him: she continues her verse as though there had been no interruption at all. Lucio's words are an interjection only, and the passage ought to be printed accordingly:

Isab.:   . . . but it is tyrannous
       To use it like a giant—
Luc.: That's well said.
Isab.:   —could great men thunder
       As Jove himself does, Jove would ne'er be quiet. . . .

How much livelier the scene becomes! Isabella does not stop and wait for Lucio's remark; she does not even hear him. All her strength of feeling is concentrated in her plea. (It is apparently this inner warmth that kindles in Angelo the fire of infatuation.) The scene gains in tempo and characterization by that uninterruptedness which Shakespeare apparently wishes.

(2)

Measure for Measure, III. 1. 145 ff.:

Isab.: I'll pray a thousand prayers for thy death,
       No word to save thee.

Claud.:   Nay, hear me, Isabel.
Isab.:   O, fie, fie, fie!
Thy sin's not accidental, but a trade. . . .

Which way have we to turn? We could make Claudio's words the second part of an iambus:

No words to save thee.—Nay, hear me, Isabel.

The result, however, would be a pause after Isabella's three-fold "fie"—and what purpose would a pause serve just where "tempo accelerando" is indispensable? Or we could make Claudio's words the first part of a new verse (as it is done in all editions):

Nay, hear me, Isabel.—O, fie, fie, fie!

But then we should have a pause after Isabella's: "No word to save thee"—and that would be equally impossible, just where Claudio tries to interrupt his sister's fulmination. Whichever turn we take, neither is satisfactory—as long as we stick to the idea that it was Shakespeare's aim to write regular iambics.

Again the solution appears to be: uninterruptedness (or: simultaneousness). Isabella works herself up into a veritable frenzy: "Die, perish!" Claudio endeavours to interrupt her, but—and that is the point—he does not succeed: Isabella's lines go on uninterruptedly:

I'll pray a thousand prayers for thy death,
No word to save thee—O, fie, fie, fie!
Thy sin's not accidental, but a trade. . . .

—while Claudio is left to intersperse his words: "Nay, hear me, Isabel" where best he can, out of rhythm and line. Again, how much livelier the passage becomes by that touch of the producer's hand!

(3)

In *Othello*, III. 3. 93 ff., the modern editions divide the lines as follows:

Iago: My noble lord—
Oth.:   What dost thou say, Iago?
Iago: Did Michael Cassio, when you woo'd my lady
    Know of your love? (————————)
Oth.: He did, from first to last: why dost thou ask?
Iago: But for a satisfaction of my thought. . . .

In this arrangement we have a pause after "Know of your love". But there a pause would be appropriate if Othello, before answering, would scan Iago's face or in whatever way show mistrust. Nothing of the sort, however, can be assumed; on the contrary, Othello, still unsuspicious, replies unhesitatingly: "He did . . ."—and thus a pause just there seems inadmissible.

I think we have to arrange the passage like this:

Iago: Did Michael Cassio, when you woo'd my lady,
    Know of your love?
Oth.:   He did, from first to last:
    Why dost thou ask? (————————)
Iago: But for a satisfaction of my thought. . . .

This line-division does away with that uncalled-for pause after "Know of your love" and is satisfactory in that it makes Othello answer the question at once. At the same time we are left with a pause after: "Why dost thou ask?"—and there I think it is in its proper place. We know by now Iago's pretence of hesitancy and cautiousness, intended to evoke Othello's curiosity and suspicion. Thus, after "Why dost thou ask?" Iago will probably shrug his shoulders or make some other gesture of blatant "casualness" in order to give the impression that his question did not mean to purport anything at all; only then he will go on:

> But for a satisfaction of my thought. . . .

In the Folio the line in question is printed like this:

> He did, from first to last:
> Why dost thou aske?
> *Iago.* But for a satisfaction of my Thought,
> No further harme.

There would have been space enough to put "Why dost thou ask?" in the same line as "He did, from first to last". None the less, the compositor set two half-lines, obviously because he found them so in the manuscript. It does not seem to go too far to assume that the author wanted to indicate the pause after "Why dost thou ask".

(4)

Lear, in I. 4. 318 ff., re-enters in full rage. Immediately before he had cursed his eldest daughter. Now, on hearing that fifty of his knights are to be dismissed, he comes back in order to say something more formidable still than his curse. In the Folio the lines read like this:

> What fiftie of my Followers at a clap?
> Within a fortnight?
> *Alb.* What's the matter Sir?
> *Lear.* Ile tell thee:
> Life and death, I am asham'd
> That thou hast power to shake my manhood
> thus. . . .

That has been arranged by the editors as follows:

> What, fifty of my followers at a clap,
> Within a fortnight?

Alb.:   What's the matter, sir?
Lear: I'll tell thee. (*To Goneril*) Life and death, I am
                                                    asham'd
          That thou hast power to shake my manhood
                                                       thus. . . .

The result of this arrangement is that Lear appears to
stop after "fortnight"; to wait until Albany has put his
question; to reply to this question, promising to let him
know his answer later; and that only then he turns to
Goneril. Theobald (1733) was the first to insert after "I'll
tell thee" the direction: "(*To Goneril*)", thus making it
clear that in his opinion the words "I'll tell thee" are not
addressed to Goneril, but to Albany. This direction we
find in all modern editions, ordinary and scholarly alike,
and in all German translations, excepting my own.

If we have any feeling for acting—or what it ought to
be—we cannot assume that Lear, just there, on the peak
of his rage and fury, struggling as he is with his own tears,
should show such an equilibrium of mind as to enable
him (a) to listen to Albany and even to hear and understand what he says, and (b) to answer him. (What, by
the way, is it that he promises to tell him?) No, if ever
there was a man blind and deaf to the rest of the world
it is Lear at this moment where he knows of nothing but
one wish: to outdo his own curse.

I think we have here another instance of uninterrupted
speech. Lear is almost overcome with emotion; his eyes
are swimming with tears: the next moment he will be
unable to stop their overflowing. He speaks to no one
else but to Goneril; for Albany he has neither eyes nor ears.

          What, fifty of my followers at a clap?
          Within a fortnight? I'll tell thee—

Here he is trying to utter something dreadful; but his
tears interrupt him, his voice fails. Swallowing down his
emotion he goes on:

> Life and death — — I am asham'd
> That thou hast power to shake my manhood **thus**
> That these hot tears . . .

I think the passage should be arranged in a way that (1) the continuance of Lear's utterances becomes visible; (2) that Albany's words appear as what they are: an interspersion only, not causing any interruption in Lear's speech and, therefore, no break in verse either; and (3) that the pauses are shown where Lear is combating his own emotion.

> Within a fortnight?
> Alb.: What's the matter, sir?
> Lear: I'll tell thee—
> Life and death — — I am asham'd
> That thou hast power to shake my manhood
>   thus. . . .

But, someone might object, what about the line:

> Within a fortnight? I'll tell thee

—is this not a deficient verse? For a good actor there will be no problem. If only his emotion has reached the appropriate temperature he will fill the line to the bursting point, either by physical means (storming up to Goneril, stopping only when face to face with her, raising his clenched fists, etc.) or by putting the whole strength of his feeling into his voice, in which case, either shouting or in a whisper of rage he would stress every syllable of "I'll tell thee":

> Within a fortnight? I'll—tell—thee—!
> $x — x — x / — — —$

Whichever way the actor may turn we may rest assured that the line will be filled with the emotion needed. Shakespeare has provided the sails; it is for the actor to fill them with his own breath. If, however, the actor is expressly told, as in effect he is by the editors: "Here you must stop your rage for a moment to let Albany interrupt you; listen to him and give him an answer; and then take up your rage again—" —no, I refuse to believe that this is the advice Shakespeare would have given his friend Burbadge.

(5)

King Lear, II. 4. 251 ff.: The two daughters reduce the number of followers whom Lear is to bring with him.

Reg.   I entreate you
      To bring but fiue and twentie, to no more
      Will I giue place or notice.
Lear. I gaue you all.
Reg. And in good time you gaue it.
Lear. Made you my Guardians, my Depositaries. . . .

This is the line-division—and also the punctuation—of the Folio. The editors' arrangement is this:

      Will I give place or notice.
Lear: I gave you all—
Reg.   And in good time you gave it.
Lear: Made you my guardians, my depositaries. . . .

In this arrangement we have a pause after "notice" where it makes no sense, the less so as Lear, on hearing the word *"give"*, at once snaps in with the same word: "I *gave* you all", in which exclamation, however, the word "I" ought to be stressed. The word "give" touches Lear's wound, and on hearing it he cries out: "Not even a handful of my followers will you give shelter: but I—didn't I give you all?"

The arrangement of the Folio, merely printed in modern fashion, seems to be more appropriate.

Will I give place or notice.

Lear: I gave you all—

Reg.: And in good time you gave it.

Lear: —made you my guardians, my depositaries. . . .

This arrangement (1) shows that Lear after "notice" actually snaps in at once; (2) it makes the actor stress the "I" in "I gave you all"; and (3) makes him speak the half-line and his next verse as one uninterrupted (or almost uninterrupted) sentence.

But then the question might arise: is Regan's sentence an "aside"? I think it is. That her words are not meant to be heard or understood by Lear is shown (a) by the fact that his words in the first and third line form in rhythm and grammar one unbroken unity, and (b) that Lear does not react to his daughter's remark. He who answers takes up and continues his partner's line; he who does not reply proceeds with his own line. That, it appears, is the case here.

Yet although Regan's words are technically an interjection only, they are too long and too important to be drowned by simultaneous speech. Lear, therefore, will have to find some device to allow Regan to utter her sarcasm audibly. He will either pronounce the word "all" a little longer, or take a deep breath after it, or do both, so that she may pour out her venom quietly and clearly. That little trick will not impair the impression of Lear's speaking uninterruptedly.

(6)

The passage in *King Lear*, IV. I. 10 ff., seems to contradict my theory that a character, after an "aside", does not continue the other speaker's line. All modern editions, including the scholarly ones, print the passage like this:

Edg.:   World, world, O world!
          But that thy strange mutations make us hate thee,
          Life would not yield to age.
Old Man: O my good lord!
          I have been your tenant, and your father's tenant,
          These fourscore years.

The Old Man is not expected to "have heard" Edgar's
soliloquy; nevertheless he is made to continue a line
broken off by Edgar. Yet he is made to do so by the
editors only, not by Shakespeare: Folio as well as Quartos
print the Old Man's words as prose. Dr. Johnson was the
first to versify them, and all the others followed suit un-
questioningly. Ben Jonson's ghost was still walking
strong at Dr. Johnson's time, and has not been laid even
yet. "Rest, rest, perturbèd spirit!"

(7)

The Quarto of *Othello*, 1622, seems to me to show
Shakespeare's original text (the same we have in the
Folio), touched up, however, by a prosodically-minded
man, brought up in the school of which Ben Jonson was
the head. Whoever he was, he must be regarded as one
of the first editors of Shakespeare. He is recognizable as
such by his enthusiasm for regularizing "faulty" lines.
I have already referred to this man on previous occasions;
here I propose to quote two more instances, in order to
show how his mind worked.
There is first the line in v. 2. 7:

          Should I repent me. But once put out thy light....
          — x x — x / x — x — x —

No doubt the line is slightly defective if we look at it not
from the actor's but the prosodist's point of view. The

editor changed "thy light" into "thine", and so the Quarto reads:

> Should I repent me; but once put out thine. . . .
> — x x — x / — x — x —

It did not matter to that pedant that, while achieving his "regularity", he succeeded in making the line stumble rather than run, having to stress "but" and "put". Pope, by the way, also regularized the line: he did so by omitting the "me"—and so in his text we find:

> Should I repent; but once put out thy light. . . .

For all of them the first commandment was: Thou shalt regularize thy author's verse!

The other instance is from the same scene, 215 ff.: Emilia, being told by Othello about the handkerchief, cries out, according to the Folio:

> Oh Heauen! oh heauenly Powres!
> *Iago.* Come, hold your peace.
> *Emil.* 'Twill out, 'twill out. I peace?
> No, I will speak as liberall as the North. . . .

That has been changed by the editor of the Quarto:

> O God, O heauenly God!
> *Iago.* Zouns, hold your peace.
> *Emil.* 'Twill out, 'twill (out): I hold my peace sir, no,
> Ile be in speaking, liberall as the ayre. . . .

The verse, so expressive of Emilia's extreme emotion:

> 'Twill out, 'twill out! I—! peace—!

with its long drawn-out vowels of "I" and "peace" seemed to that editor to need correction. So he corrected —and since, in order to do so, he had transferred the "No" from the second to the first line, he had to reshape the second line, too. Also the "ayre" seemed to him to

84

be more "liberall" than the "North". Dr. Johnson decided for the Quarto and most of the editors have followed his example.

After this introduction, intended to show the sort of problems the editor of the Quarto evidently thought he had to deal with, I turn to the passage II. I. 200 ff.

While Othello embraces and kisses his wife, Iago has a short soliloquy:

> And this, and this the greatest discords be
> That e'er our hearts shall make. [Embrace.]
> Iago: Oh, you are well tun'd now: but I'll set down the
>   pegs that make that music, as honest as I am.
> Oth.: Come: let us to the castle. [He starts leading her
>   away. Stopping and turning round.]
>   News, friends, our wars are done: [Pause of ex-
>   pectation.]
>   The Turks are drown'd. [General cheering.]
>   How does my old acquaintance of this isle?

The editor of the Quarto, however, thought it inadmissible that Iago should speak prose when Othello speaks verse (although before and afterwards Iago speaks nothing but prose)—and so he versified the passage. Rowe, Pope, Theobald, and Warburton stuck to the prose of the Folio, but all the others followed the Quarto, with the result that in all modern editions the passage reads like this:

> That e'er our hearts shall make.
> Iago: O, you are well tun'd now!
> But I'll set down the pegs that make this music,
> As honest as I am.
> Oth.:   Come, let us to the castle.
> News, friends; our wars are done, the Turks are
>   drown'd.
> How does my old acquaintance of this isle?

We have to keep in mind that Ben Jonson had published his own Folio only six years before; considering the reputation the poet laureate enjoyed in his day we cannot wonder that the editor of the Quarto thought it his duty to bring Shakespeare's poetical diction as close as possible to that of Ben Jonson.

In the present case he did not, as in so many other instances, interfere with the text as such. He contented himself with letting Iago speak verse, not bothering about the fact that the verse thus manufactured has six feet:

> That e'er our hearts shall make.—O, you are well
> tun'd now!

The same is the case with the "verse":

> As honest as I am.—Come, let us to the castle.

Yet the worst, in my opinion, is that he made Othello continue Iago's broken-off "verse", although the latter's words are an obvious "aside". Should Othello really continue the metrical scheme of a speech he has "not heard", he would make havoc of my whole theory. I hope I have shown, however, that here I am up not against Shakespeare, but against that unknown grammarian who in well-meaning ardour wanted Shakespeare's versification to appear as clean and polished as that of John Ford or Ben Jonson.

In my conviction it is in the Folio that we have the genuine text of *Othello*. We should not allow ourselves to be led astray by an editor who evidently was no theatrical man and did not, therefore, understand why and in which ways Shakespeare's diction differs from that of his fellow-playwrights.

(8)

In *Twelfth-Night*, I. 5. 295 ff., the accepted text is divided like this:

Viola: O, you should not rest
       Between the elements of air and earth,
       But you should pity me. (————— —————)
Oliv.: You might do much. What is your parentage?
Viola: Above my fortunes, yet my state is well:
       I am a gentleman.
Oliv.:   Get you to your lord. . . .

Why should Olivia make that long pause before she
says: "You might do much"? A better arrangement
would be this:

       But you should pity me.
Oliv.:   You might do much.
       What is your parentage? (————————)
Viola: Above my fortunes, yet my state is well:
       I am a gentleman.

In this arrangement we have a pause after the question,
and there it is where it ought to be. The inquiry about
her parentage takes Viola by surprise: what is she to
answer? Of course she must hesitate for a moment, turn
half away, or look sideways, or whatever the actress might
do to show her slight embarrassment, before she collects
herself and replies with that non-committal answer:
"Above my fortunes . . .".
Proof that the line-division as suggested by me is
correct seems to be provided a few lines further on.
Olivia, left to herself, quotes both question and answer;
they are verbally repeated, and there they are actually
arranged like this:

       What is your parentage? (————— —————)
       Above my fortunes, yet my state is well:
       I am a gentleman.

—including the pause after "parentage".

(9)

Hamlet, II. 2. 150 ff.: Polonius sums up what he thinks are the reasons and symptoms of Hamlet's madness. In all editions we find the passage arranged like this:

> Into the madness wherein now he raves,
> And all we wail for.
> King: Do you think 'tis this?
> Queen: It may be, very likely.
> Polon.: Hath there been such a time—I'd fain know
>   that—

Should this be the correct line-division we should have the King reply at once; on the other hand there would, after the Queen's answer, be a pause before Polonius goes on. Either seems unlikely, if only from the psychological point of view.

Surely the King will ponder for a moment on what he has heard; he will perhaps meaningly look at his Queen —between themselves they know more of the matter— and only then will he put his question. As to Polonius, it is improbable that this chatterbox should let pass a single moment before uttering one of his ever-ready remarks and observations. The following arrangement seems to meet both demands:

> Into the madness wherein now he raves,
> And all we wail for. (————————————)
> King: Do you think 'tis this?
> Queen: It may be, very likely.
> Polon.: Hath there been such a time—I'd fain know that—

(10)

In *Hamlet*, I. I. 35 ff., the Folio arranges the lines as follows:

88

Barn. Last night of all,
   When yond same Starre, that's Westward from the
                                                    Pole
   Had made his course t'illume that part of Heauen
   Where now it burnes, Marcellus and my selfe,
   The Bell then beating one.
Mar. Peace, breake thee of: *Enter the Ghost.*
   Looke where it comes againe.
Barn. In the same figure, like the King that's dead.

In all modern editions the last four lines are arranged
like this:

   The bell then beating one—
Mar.: Peace! break thee off; look where it comes again!
      (*Enter Ghost.*)
Bern.: In the same figure, like the king that's dead.

It is not only the line-division, but also the entry of
the Ghost I propose to examine.

After "Last night of all" there is a pause. Bernardo
turns round to find the star to which he wishes to refer;
he probably points to it. The theatrical purpose is
obvious: it is to draw Horatio's (and the audience's) attention away from the door through which the Ghost is to
enter in a few seconds. Marcellus, not interested in
Bernardo's story, because he was present last night himself, watches that door apprehensively; this is shown by
the fact that he is the first to see the apparition. He
interrupts Bernardo: "Peace, break thee off!"

At this point we should expect that, as Marcellus interrupts his partner, he should continue his verse. And so
he does. If ever there was a line that must not be broken
off it is this (despite Bernardo's being told to "break off").
A pause after: "The bell then beating one" is impossible.
The passage ought to be arranged like this:

89

> Where now it burns, Marcellus and myself,
> The bell then beating one—

Mar.:   Peace, break thee off!

> *(Enter the Ghost.)*
> Look where it comes again.

Bern.: In the same figure, like the king that's dead.

In this arrangement we have a pause after: "Look, where it comes again"—and there the pause is placed where, from the producer's point of view, a pause is indispensable. Marcellus sees the Ghost; he commands silence (hissing his: "Peace, break thee off!")—the two jump up from the floor where they were sitting—all three retire as far as possible in a frightened scramble—and now they stare, "distill'd almost to jelly", at the walking apparition. Certainly a little while of tense watching must be assumed to pass before Bernardo whispers:

> In the same figure, like the king that's dead.

The question remains where the entry of the Ghost should be indicated. All editors prior to Edward Dowden put "Enter the Ghost" after: "Look where it comes again"—where it is too late. Professor Dowden (in *The Arden Shakespeare*) made him enter after: "The bell then beating one"—which I think is too early. Professor J. Dover Wilson (in *The New Shakespeare*, Cambridge) follows Dowden's example.

What is the situation on the stage? The three are waiting for the moment that for Shakespeare, the producer, must have been one of the most crucial of his whole career: the appearance of the Ghost. The moment was difficult not only because of the daylight, in which it is awkward for a spectre to walk, and because all the helps of a modern stage were lacking, but chiefly because the Ghost had to appear as early as in the first scene of the play: an unknown figure, never seen before. When

Banquo's Ghost appears, or Cæsar's, we recognize them at once as what they now are, since we know they have been killed. Here it is different, and Shakespeare was confronted with the task of preventing his audience from the otherwise normal assumption that the figure that was next to emerge from the tiring-house was just another ordinary character in the play. How does he solve that problem?

First he creates a verbal night. Not only is it so dark that the sentinels find it hard to recognize each other, ("Who's there?", etc.) but there are seven verbal indications of night:

> 'Tis now struck twelve . . . get thee to bed . . . good night . . . Give you good night . . . good night . . . appear'd again to-night? . . . the minutes of this night. . . .

Then he makes them speak of the Ghost:

> . . . has this thing appear'd again . . . seen nothing . . . but our fantasy . . . will not believe . . . this dreaded sight . . . twice seen . . . this apparition . . . approve our eyes and speak to it . . . tush, 'twill not appear.

How cunning a preparation! How crafty a mixture of "appear, see, sight, thing, apparition, belief, dread, eyes, fantasy" and again "seen, appear". Then he makes the two sit down—on the floor of course—and Bernardo begins his story. By that trick with the star, attention is deflected from the entrance—and before Bernardo in his hushed and somewhat involved report has yet reached the verb of his sentence, Marcellus whispers his warning: "Peace, break thee off!" They jump to their feet, stumble back, and in horror-stricken silence stare towards the entrance.

Seen in that light it seems clear why Shakespeare

wishes Horatio and Bernardo to be seated. It is not, as Prof. Dover Wilson suggests, because Horatio is bored, but because the way in which the actors jump up, stagger back, and cling together in a horrified group, shows their panic far more impressively than had they been standing all the time.

That leads to a point that Shakespeare obviously regarded as very important; for it is evident that he did his best to bring it off. He did so by his line-division and by putting the Ghost's entry where, in the Folio, it stands. That point is that he wanted the three to see the apparition before the audience become aware of it. He wishes the three to reel back from the approaching spectre: when in that dramatic way the "dreaded sight" is heralded—by the shadow as it were that it casts before—only then the Ghost himself enters. The wave of horror that goes forth from the walking corpse is to seize first the three on the stage and only then to sweep on to the audience. It is the effect the apparition has on those three that, more than anything else, convinces the onlookers that the approaching figure is not of this world.

That method of delegated effect, i.e. showing the effect not directly but on intermediaries who act as reflecting mirrors, is an old device. Homer uses it when he lets us gauge Helen's beauty by describing the effect she has on the old men that sit on the wall while she passes by. In "Don Giovanni" Leporello, having looked outside, comes reeling back, terrified at the approaching monster, and only when in this way we have been prepared for what is to come does the walking monument itself appear. The same trick, after all, is used in Horatio's incredulity: "Tush, tush, 'twill not appear!" He does not believe in ghosts; nor do the hearers, so far. Now, however, when he, the audience's outpost, is converted so completely, must not they feel converted themselves?

In a modern production the difference between the

Dowden-Wilson and the Folio version as to when the Ghost is to enter would not be too great. Present-day stage mechanism can do much to let the Ghost appear in a convincingly ghost-like manner. For Shakespeare it was a different matter. That man had to move on to the stage, armed from top to toe, a truncheon in his hand, on his head a helmet, "his beaver up", with a grizzled beard: for all his outer appearance just another human being. What could the producer do to indicate that this particular figure is coming from that undiscovered country? With a little white paint he could make him look "very pale" (I. 2.); that was all. Beside that, he had to rely on merely histrionic means by which to transform a walking man into a ghost. To change the circumstances of this man's entry is to ignore the producer in Shakespeare. Why not stick to what the Folio says? Why not trust the compositors with the ability to transfer into print what they found in the manuscript? And why not believe that he who wrote that script knew his job?

VIII

"THE BLEEDING SERGEANT"

IN chapters VI and VII I have purposely abstained from quoting any instances from *Macbeth*, the reason being that I wanted to deal with that play separately—which I propose now to do in the following pages.

It seems to me that the text of *Macbeth* is the only one of which we may assume with any measure of certainty that it shows no traces of "editorial" interference. I feel convinced that the texts of many, if not most, of the other plays have been "regularized" either before they were set up in print or during that process. The later editors, consequently, were startled and puzzled when they had to deal with the text of *Macbeth*. Comparing it with the other texts they did not come to the conclusion that the latter may have been tampered with (in a similar way as the editor of the Quarto 1622 tampered with the text of *Othello*) and that just the one before them may have retained its original shape. On the contrary: as literary men, brought up with that tenet of "regularity first", they concluded that this text must have been badly preserved, worse than that of any other play. Thus it is that just *Macbeth* (probably the only play from which the real yard-stick of Shakespeare's diction can be obtained) has been put into the Procrustean bed of "regularization". Whole scenes have been mutilated by the cruel procedure of cutting lines and transposing them higher up or lower down—for no other reason than that of satisfying, not Shakespeare's, but the editors' own poetical demand, i.e. the demand of continuity of versification. What by way of worshipping that fetish has been done cries to heaven.

It has been suggested—and in complete seriousness—
(by W. G. Clark and W. A. Wright, editors of the play
in the *Clarendon Press*, and by Henry Cuningham, its
editor in *The Arden Shakespeare*) that the first scenes of
Macbeth (I. I. and I. 2. and the first 37 lines of I. 3.) were
not written by Shakespeare. "The slovenly metre is not
like his work." They assume that "Shakespeare reserved
to himself all the scenes in which Macbeth or Lady
Macbeth appeared, but left the rest to his assistant".
Mr. Cuningham maintains that a mere comparison of
I. 2. with what he calls the authentic opening of the play
(I. 3. 38 ff.) "ought to be sufficient to convince any reader
whose ear is not too indurated or elongated for the
adequate comprehension of Shakespeare's blank verse,
that Shakespeare's hand never rested here". Should
we still believe in the authenticity of I. I. and I. 2.,
then, he goes on, "the first act . . . was begun by
Shakespeare drunk and continued by Shakespeare
sober".

I do not hesitate to call all that sheer nonsense. Nor
do I feel any doubt about the genuineness of the Hecate
scene, III. 5. Apart from all other considerations, those
scenes are indispensable, if only for their structural purpose. Without the two preceding appearances of the
witches and their self-revelations no one in the Globe
theatre would have understood what the three creatures
really are who suddenly confront Macbeth and Banquo.
Nor would the witches' scene in IV. I. have been feasible
without due preparation. It is this purpose of preparation that underlies those scenes.

In considering them we must, first of all, forget that
we have read the play before, and imagine instead the
position in which the audience found themselves when
listening to the first performance, i.e. knowing nothing
whatsoever of what they were waiting to see. We, it is
true, might be able to do without the first scenes in which

the weird sisters disclose who they are; but that audience could not: for them, it was obviously necessary to be told. For us, it is not difficult, by means of artificial darkness, electric fire, etc., to make the witches' kitchen plausible; but Shakespeare himself was in a different position: his cauldron did not seethe, his fire did not burn, his cavern was not dark. His apparitions, the Crowned Child, etc., had to pop out their heads by the trap-door and there to disappear again—in broad daylight. All Shakespeare could do was to tell his audience beforehand what they were going to see; only then, trusting their ears more than their eyes, they saw what they were wanted to see—in their imagination. To assume that Shakespeare could have done without those scenes, in which he, as it were, switched on his hearers' imagination, shows complete forgetfulness of the limitations of his stage.

I propose to deal first with the scene I. 2., and only with its beginning, i.e. the short scene with the "Bleeding Sergeant". I choose this scene because those editors have been so shocked by its "slovenly metre" and its "numerous faulty lines which deface it" that, not content to call it "worthlessly corrupt", they go so far as to say "that it is the interpolator—generally supposed to be Middleton —and *not* Shakespeare who is responsible for the 'bleeding sergeant' "

Dunc.: What bloody man is that? He can report,
　　　　As seemeth by his plight, of the revolt
　　　　The newest state.
Malc.: 　　　　　　　　　　This is the sergeant
　　　　Who like a good and hardy soldier fought
　　　　'Gainst my captivity: Hail, brave friend;
　　　　Say to the king the knowledge of the broil,
　　　　As thou didst leave it.
Capt.: Doubtful it stood—
　　　　As two spent swimmers, that do cling together. . . .

(a)

The metre of line 3, say the *Clarendon* editors, would
be regular, if "sergeant" were pronounced as a trisyllable
—and Abbott, in paragraph 479, actually suggests that
we should pronounce it so:

The new-/est state./This is/the ser-/ge-ant. . . .
x — x — x — x — x —

Dover Wilson too maintains, in his Notes, that *sergeant*
is "three syllables".

But the line becomes, if not "regular", at least natural if
we allow for the gap between "state" and "This" that is
evidently called for by the situation. The King asks.
Before answering, surely Malcolm must have a look at the
man, especially as he is bleeding and probably led by a
comrade or two. That short moment of looking and making
sure causes, or is indicated by, that gap. Such a pause is
certainly good acting, better than what is usually done on
the stage: that Malcolm simply waits for his cue and
replies at once as though he knew the answer even before
asked. Shakespeare in any case wanted the pause—or he
would not have made it in the verse.

(b)

'Gainst my captivity: Hail, brave friend. . . .

"Here again", the *Clarendon* editors say, "the metre
is imperfect." And so says Dover Wilson. True,
before "Hail" one syllable is missing; but it is obvious
that here, too, the gap is caused, and appropriately
filled in, by action. Malcolm has spoken to his
father; now he turns to address the bleeding man. For
this turn, for a step or two in his direction, or simply for
a jerk of his head, we should, after all the instances we
have seen before, expect a small pause: and there it is.

Moreover, before "Hail" we have a colon (not in the editions, to be sure, but in the Folio). In certain plays, among them *Macbeth*, the colon almost always stands for a gesture. On this point, however, I shall have to say more later on.

(c)

As thou didst leave it.
Capt.: Doubtful it stood—
    As two spent swimmers, that do cling together. . . .

All editors share the opinion that the two half-lines:

As thou didst leave it.—Doubtful it stood. . . .

are meant to form one iambic. To improve its metre, Pope read: "Doubtful long it stood", and Steevens suggested we should read: "Doubtfully it stood".

Yet the question is whether Shakespeare really wishes the Sergeant to continue Malcolm's line. Is it not dramatically more probable that the man, who drags himself along painfully, could not have his reply ready and prepared? Would he not rather first stop, slowly raise his head, and gaze at the enquirer before starting to speak? Would he not after: "Doubtful it stood" pause for a while and collect himself, searching for the right word, before he gets under way with his story? Would not that be better acting? It would in any case account for the two pauses which, I think, are indicated by the broken versification.

(d)

The Captain's report has been blamed as being incoherent and ungrammatical, hardly yielding to attempts at regularization. So it really is. Yet what are the conclusions we are to draw from that fact? That its author

98

was not able to write regular and grammatically coherent speech? That the author, therefore, cannot be Shakespeare? Or is there a different explanation from the dramatist's point of view?

What the editors call "anomalies of speech" are in reality artistic means of expression. Anomalous are the man's conditions and his anomalous speech conforms to them—or, to express it more correctly: the anomaly of his speech is an indication of his anomalous conditions. He is wounded, exhausted, on the verge of breaking down. He cannot be expected to speak in well-set phrases, carefully begun and completed. One needs only to punctuate his lines as a modern playwright would, and one can almost see, as expressed in his broken-off sentences, how he gasps for breath and finds it difficult to keep himself upright.

> Doubtful it stood——
> As two spent swimmers, that do cling together,
> And choke their art—the merciless Macdonwald—
> Worthy to be a rebel—for to that—
> The multiplying villanies of nature
> Do swarm upon him—from the western isles
> Of Kernes and Gallowglasses is supplied. . . .

(e)

Shortly afterwards the Folio prints Duncan's question:

> Dismay'd not this our captains, Macbeth and
> Banquo?

as what it is—prose. Shakespeare wishes to bring in the two names. A line with proper names, however, is sometimes a little difficult to versify—and Shakespeare did not bother about it. Yet the editors thought he ought to have bothered—and so we find the lines arranged like this:

> Began a fresh assault.
>
> King: Dismay'd not this
> Our captains, Macbeth and Banquo?
>
> Capt.:   Yes;
> As sparrows eagles, or the hare the lion.

Still, the verse does not read as verse. To improve its metre the *Clarendon* editors suggest—as does Abbott—that the verse should be "made regular" by pronouncing "captains" as "capitains"—and Sidney Walker proposed: "Our captains twain".

(f)

In the Captain's reply (as printed in the Folio):

> Yes, as Sparrowes, Eagles;
> Or the Hare, the Lyon:

the word "yes" stands outside the metrical scheme:

> Yes,
> As sparrows eagles, or the hare the lion!

It is an ironical interjection—such as "Ah!"—and is probably accompanied by a contemptuous laugh. Why should it be squeezed into the verse when its real purpose is to interrupt the verse?

We find a similar irregularity a few lines later:

> So they doubly redoubled stroakes vpon the Foe:

Most editions show the following arrangement:

> So they
> Doubly redoubled strokes upon the foe.

In this case the editors are right. For there certainly is a pause after "So they", and it seems obvious what it implies. The Captain probably stretches himself to his full length, raises his sword to demonstrate how the two heroes dealt with their enemies, and then, his sword coming down heavily, he breaks out in grim triumph, starting with a heavy dactyl:

Doubly redoubled strokes upon the foe!

(g)

Or memorize another Golgotha
I cannot tell: but I am faint—
My gashes cry for help——

This passage (with the gap in the second verse, caused by the man's exhausted stumble, and with the pause in the last line) I have dealt with in Chapter IV (11). I only draw attention to the colon after "I cannot tell", left out or changed by all editors: here, too, the colon serves as an indication for a gesture.

★

Summing up, I find it impossible to imagine any "interpolator" or "assistant" who would have been able to write this episode of the "Bleeding Sergeant". The gaps and pauses found there are unmistakable hall-marks of the master's forge, and the craftsmanship with which the Captain's exhaustion is characterized by his manner of speaking is unsurpassed by anything we can find even in Shakespeare's best plays. And yet during three centuries the editors were bewildered by what they should have admired as an apex and marvel of dramatic expressiveness.

It is the lack of regularity in the versification and the untidiness of the Captain's language that has irritated the editors. In both aspects they would find themselves satisfied with a highly "poetical" version of the scene as given in the translation, or adaptation, of *Macbeth* by Schiller. He was indeed a poet after their own heart: he strictly adhered to the rules of prosody and grammar. In his *Macbeth* he first of all made the Sergeant a Knight—

and this is how he makes him speak. In my (re-)translation I am accurate also as to the complete lack of pauses, gaps, and other "anomalies" of diction.

King: Look, there they lead a knight straight from the
                                                battle.
        Now we shall hear the outcome of the fight.
Malc.: This is the selfsame knight who fought for me,
        Or else I'd have been taken prisoner.
        Welcome, my fellow-warrior! Tell the King:
        How did the battle stand when thou didst leave it?
Knight: For long it had been swaying to and fro,
        As though two swimmers, clinging to each other,
        In single combat prove their skill and strength.

King: Did not that frighten our two generals,
        Macbeth and Banquo?
Knight: Well, as sparrows frighten
        The sovereign eagle, or a roe, the lion.
        They did not waste much time to wipe the sweat
        From their hot brows, but tried their luck once
                                                more
        In a new fight, and when I left the field
        The armies were engaged in a sharp clash.
        More, sir, I cannot tell; I am completely
        Exhausted, and my wounds demand attention.

Here, nothing is irregular, neither the metre nor the grammar. Everybody replies in orderly diction and in perfect uninterruptedness. In the end, the Knight makes the statement that he is "completely exhausted". He says so and so we must believe him. But does he show it in his manner of speaking? Does he, weak and wounded as he is, express himself differently from a man who is strong and unhurt? Not in the least. The "Bleeding Sergeant" does, and because he does so the editors declare that they "cannot recognize Shakespeare's hand having ever rested there" and speak of "adulterating trash" which "the un-thinking reader is still allowed to go on reading as if it sprang from Shakespeare's lawful parentage".

However, apart from attempts at regularizing metre and punctuation, those editors could not interfere with the language itself. The German translators could—and did: following their English masters, they regarded the Captain's report as "un-Shakespearian" and "corrected" it accordingly. True, none of them went as far as Schiller, who, with his lofty conception of the poet's calling, "ennobled" everything he touched, raising it to a "higher level". All the same, with Schiller's ideas before their eyes the translators thought it their duty to avoid all pauses, gaps, and other "irregularities" and, in the Captain's case, to "ennoble" his speech—little aware that by doing so they obliterated just what distinguishes a mere poet from a dramatic writer. Schiller's diction is poetical; Shakespeare's, dramatic. Schiller endows all his characters with his own diction; however many mouths there are, from each one we hear the voice of the poet himself. Shakespeare's voice we do not hear at all; his characters speak each in his own way—and an exhausted man speaks in an exhausted manner.

IX

PAUSES IN "MACBETH"

(1)

III. 4. 11 ff, (with the line-division of the Folio):

Macb.: Be large in mirth, anon we'll drink a measure
The table round. (————————————)
There's blood upon thy face.
Murd.: 'Tis Banquo's, then.
Macb.: 'Tis better thee without than he within.
Is he dispatch'd?
Murd.: My lord, his throat is cut,
That I did for him.
Macb.: Thou art the best o'th' cut-throats,
Yet he's good that did the like for Fleance.
If thou didst it, thou art the nonpareil
Murd.: Most royal sir (————————————)
Fleance is 'scap'd.
Macb.: Then comes my fit again:
I had else been perfect. . . .

The give and take of conversation is interrupted twice, i.e. we have two pauses. The first occurs after: "The table round". Here Macbeth walks away from the banquet and towards the Murderer, who cannot well join the party. Most editors, rightly though unnecessarily, insert the stage-direction: "(Approaching the door)"; but in the verse they do not allow for the pause needed for that approaching.

The second pause is after: "Most royal sir". Here the Folio arranges the lines like this:

Most Royall Sir
Fleans is scap'd.

There we have two indications of the pause: first the gap in metre, clearly showing after "Sir"; the second hint lies in the absence of any punctuation after "Sir"—a blank that obviously stands for a dash. What is the meaning of this pause?

The Murderer was just boasting of his skill and efficiency and Macbeth paid him a handsome tribute: "you are the best of your trade". Then, however, he goes on: "but he, too, is good who disposed of Fleance: if it is you who did it, then you are the champion". In this, however, the Murderer has to disappoint his master: "Most royal sir——" and here he hesitates, raises his shoulders, perhaps scratches his head, or in whatever way he delays his answer, before he blurts out: "Fleance is 'scap'd".

In "Yet he's good" the word "he's" has the length of two syllables; in the Folio it is printed as "hee's". Stressed, as Shakespeare apparently wishes it to be stressed, it is tantamount to: "he, too".

In all modern editions, however, including Dover Wilson's, we find the passage arranged like this:

Macb.: Be large in mirth; anon we'll drink a measure
     The table round. (*Approaching the door.*) There's
                        blood upon thy face.
Murd.: 'Tis Banquo's, then. (————————)
Macb.: 'Tis better thee without than he within.
     Is he dispatch'd? (————————)
Murd.: My lord, his throat is cut; that I did for him.
Macb.: Thou art the best o' the cut-throats; yet he's good
     That did the like for Fleance: if thou didst it,
     Thou art the nonpareil.
Murd.:   Most royal sir,
     Fleance is 'scap'd. (————————)
Macb.: Then comes my fit again; I had else been perfect. . . .

First we see that, in order to obliterate two pauses, the

editors have succeeded in creating three pauses—for two that make perfect sense, three pauses that make no sense at all. Why should Macbeth, having heard: " 'Tis Banquo's, then" pause before replying: " 'Tis better thee without . . ."? Why should the Murderer, asked about Banquo's "dispatch", hesitate before giving the proud answer that "his throat is cut"? And why, finally, should Macbeth after: "Fleance is 'scap'd" not react at once with his reply: "Then comes my fit again"?

Yet, it might be said, neither of the two actors would in fact make those pauses, since, for them, interruption of the verse does not indicate any pause at all. There can be no doubt that they are right in not seeing any meaning in the pauses that the editors have made; but it is a great pity that, misled by such arbitrary line-division, the actors do not know anything about the pauses made by Shakespeare himself—made with the obvious aim of coaching them in their acting.

Nor is that all. Within two lines the editors have succeeded in getting two stresses wrong. In the Folio full emphasis lies on: "Yet *hee's* good", while in the editors' arrangement we have the stresses: "*yet* he's *good*". In the next line the Folio has: "If *thou* didst it", with the obvious meaning: "Should it be you who did that also . . .". The editors, however, want the actor to stress the words like this: "*If* thou *didst* it . . .". But surely there is a difference between: "If *thou* didst it" and "If thou *didst* it"?

(2)

III. 4. 46 ff.:

Macb.: The table's full.
Lenn.:   Here is a place reserv'd, sir.
Macb.: Where?

Lenn.:   Here, my good lord. (————————)
          What is't that moves your highness? (————)
Macb.: Which of you have done this?
Lords: What, my good lord?
Macb.: Thou canst not say I did it: never shake . . .

Two pauses. The first, a long one, after: "Here, my good lord": Macbeth staggers back from the apparition, gasping. No doubt, there must be a pause before Lennox, frightened at the King's behaviour, puts his question. Macbeth, on the other hand, does not hear Lennox's words; he, therefore, does not continue the verse broken off by Lennox, but starts a new one: "Which of you have done this?"

Here once more Shakespeare clearly indicates the pause which he wishes the actor to make, i.e. the pause after: "Here, my good lord"; he does so by making Lennox start a new line in exactly the same way as, in the previous passage, after: "Most royal sir".

> Heere my good Lord.
> What is't that moues your Highnesse?

Can anyone believe that this line-division has come about by mere chance or by negligence either on the author's or compositor's part?

In all modern editions, however, the passage reads like this:

Macb.: The table's full.
Lenn.:   Here is a place reserv'd, sir.
Macb.: Where? (————————————)
Lenn.: Here, my good lord. What is't that moves your
                                highness?
Macb.: Which of you have done this?
Lords: What, my good lord?
Macb.: Thou canst not say I did it: never shake . . .

The pause after: "Here, my good lord", so indispensable for the producer, the pause in which Macbeth, horrified, stares at Banquo's Ghost, this pause has been obliterated; instead, we have a big gap after "Where?". There it does not make any sense at all.

X

SIMULTANEOUSNESS IN "MACBETH"?

THERE is no passage of real simultaneousness such as that
in *Hamlet*, or in *Othello*. Two short passages, however,
occur, the first in II. 3. 70 ff.

(1)

Macduff enters, having seen the murdered Duncan in
his chamber. The passage should be arranged like this:

> O horror, horror, horror,
> Tongue nor heart cannot conceive nor name thee.
> Macb. and Lenn.: What's the matter?
> Macd.: Confusion now hath made his masterpiece:
> Most sacrilegious murder hath broke ope
> The Lord's anointed temple, and stole thence
> The life o' th' building.
> Macb.: What is't you say, the life?
> Lenn.: Mean you his majesty?
> Macd.: Approach the chamber, and destroy your sight . . .

The first question: "What's the matter?" is expressly
given to both Macbeth and Lennox: they speak simultaneously. Yet their words are an interjection only, as
seen by the fact that Macduff does not interrupt his speech.
The same simultaneity, however, must be assumed in the
second case, where the two ask separate questions, and
yet certainly at the same time. That is shown by the fact
that either continues the line broken off by Macduff and
that Macduff. this time answering, begins with a new line.

(2)

In III. 4. 95 ff., Macbeth rails at Banquo's Ghost:

Thou hast no speculation in those eyes
Which thou dost glare with.

Lady M.:   Think of this, good peers,
But as a thing of custom: 'tis no other,
Only it spoils the pleasure of the time.

Macb.:   What man dare, I dare: -
Approach thou like the rugged Russian bear. . . .

The half-line: "Which thou dost glare with" is continued by both, by the Lady with: "Think of this, good peers . . ." and by Macbeth himself with: "What man dare . . .". While he, without interrupting himself, goes on challenging the apparition she tries to assuage her guests' amazement: they speak simultaneously.

All the same, had I to produce the scene I should ask Macbeth to draw out the vowels in "What man dare, I dare" as long as possible: during the two long "dare" the Lady could easily finish her quickly spoken lines so that the impression of simultaneous speech would be given rather than actual simultaneousness.

(3)

In I. 3. 127 ff., Macbeth stands by himself on one side of the stage, on the other Banquo with the two messengers. Macbeth soliloquizes, and the others are not expected to "hear" him. And yet he and Banquo seem to take up the lines broken off by the other. In point of fact, however, each continues his own speech, which he merely interrupts for a while to allow his partner to go on speaking. It is a case not so much of simultaneous speech but rather of what might be called "overlapping" speech. The following arrangement may show what I mean:

Macbeth:
That function is smother'd in surmise
And nothing is, but what is not.
     Banquo:
    Look, how our partner's rapt—
Macbeth:
If chance will have me king, why, chance may crown me,
Without my stir;
     Banquo:
           —new honours come upon him
    Like our strange garments, cleave not to their mould
    But with the aid of use.
Macbeth:
           —come what come may,
Time and the hour runs through the roughest day.

XI

VERSE, PECULIAR TO "MACBETH"

THERE is yet another point that makes the editors speak of the "corruptness" of the text: the fact that the text of *Macbeth* contains so large a number of four-foot iambics. For this there are, I think, two reasons, a general and a special one.

(A)

Beginning with the beginning of blank verse, with Marlowe's "mighty line", and following it up to our own day, we see that it has always been the trend of the English iambus to loosen its inherent stiffness by getting rid of the fifth foot and walking, dancing, or storming along rather on four legs—which after all is far more natural.

Marlowe:

O thou art fairer than the evening air
— x x — x / x x — x —

Clad in the beauty of a thousand stars
— x x — x /x x — x —

No sleep can fasten on my watchful eyes
x — x — x / x x — x —

Now lie the Christians bathing in their bloods
x — x — x / — x x x —

Discomfited in all the Christian host
x — x x x — / x — x —

Pope:

> True ease in writing comes from art, not chance
> x — x — x / x x — x —

Keats:

> Much have I travell'd in the realms of gold
> — x x — x / x x — x —

The more musical a poet, the more he feels urged by his sense of symmetry to relieve the rigidity of his verse. That is why in Shakespeare that tendency is stronger than in any other poet.

> Shall I compare thee to a summer's day?
> — x x — x / x x — x —
>
> Can I go forward when my heart is here?
> — x x — x / x x — x —
>
> The quality of mercy is not strain'd
> x — x x x — x / — x —
>
> The king hath happily receiv'd, Macbeth
> x —.x — x x x — x —
>
> Is this a dagger; which I see before me
> x — x — x / x x — x — x
>
> Most potent, grave, and reverend signiors
> x — x / — / x — x x x —
>
> So please you, something touching the Lord Hamlet
> x — x / — x / — x x x — x
>
> The sanctity and health of the whole state
> x — x x x — / x x — — —

Out of the thirty-three lines of "To be, or not to be" only ten lines, as I think they should be scanned, are genuine five-foot iambics; the remaining are four-stress lines.

The matter becomes somewhat complicated if—especially in a line with four stresses—two consecutive syllables are equally accented, as in the verse, just quoted, from *Hamlet*, I. 3. 21:

> The sanctity and health of the whole state
> x — x x x — / x x — —

The following lines are taken from one scene (III. 3.) of *Othello:*

350:

> Farewell the plumed troops and the big wars
> x — x — x — / x x — —

352:

> Farewell the neighing steed and the shrill trump
> x — x — x — / x x — —

356:

> And, O you mortal engines, whose rude throats
> x — x — x — x x — —

437:

> I gave her such a one: 'twas my first gift
> x — x — x — / x x — —

I think we are justified in assuming that in Shakespeare's blank verse there are instances where at the end as well as at the beginning of the line (and not only in the middle) two stressed syllables may clash. We may then turn to the following examples:

A Midsummer-Night's Dream, II. I. 7:

> Swifter than the moon's sphere
> — x — x — —

A Midsummer-Night's Dream, IV. I. 102:

> Trip we after the night's shade
> — x — x x — —

Doct. I haue too Nights watch'd with you, but can perceiue no truth in your report. When was it shee laſt walk'd?

Gent. Since his Maieſty went into the Field, I haue ſeene her riſe from her bed, throw her Night-Gown vppon her, vnlocke her Cloſſet, take foorth paper, folde it, write vpon't, read it, afterwards Seale it, and againe returne to bed; yet all this while in a moſt faſt ſleepe.

Doct. A great perturbation in Nature, to receyue at once the benefit of ſleep, and do the effects of watching. In this ſlumbry agitation, beſides her walking, and other actuall performances, what (at any time) haue you heard her ſay?

Gent. That Sir, which I will not report after her.

Doct. You may to me, and 'tis moſt meet you ſhould.

Gent. Neither to you, nor any one, hauing no witneſſe to confirme my ſpeech.   *Enter Lady, with a Taper.*
Lo you, heere ſhe comes: This is her very guiſe, and vpon my life faſt aſleepe: obſerue her, ſtand cloſe.

Doct. How came ſhe by that light?

Gent. Why it ſtood by her: ſhe ha's light by her continually, 'tis her command.

Doct. You ſee her eyes are open.

Gent. I but their ſenſe are ſhut.

Doct. What is it ſhe do's now?
Looke how ſhe rubbes her hands.

Gent. It is an accuſtom'd action with her, to ſeeme thus waſhing her hands: I haue knowne her continue in this a quarter of an houre.

Lad. Yet heere's a ſpot.

Doct. Heark, ſhe ſpeaks, I will ſet downe what comes from her, to ſatisfie my remembrance the more ſtrongly.

La. Out damned ſpot: out I ſay. One: Two: Why then 'tis time to doo't: Hell is murky. Fye, my Lord, fie, a Souldier, and affear'd? what need we feare? who knowes it, when none can call our powre to accompt: yet who

FIRST FOLIO, Tragedies, p. 148a. After "What is it she do's now?" the line, though prose, is not continued. The author-producer wants to make sure that we perceive what the Lady is doing. After that question there is a pause, equivalent to a stage-direction, in which he wishes the audience to watch her action. Only then does he make the Doctor add the explanation: "Looke how she rubbes her hands."

This Comoedie was firſt
Aĉted, in the yeere
1598.

By the then L. CHAMBERLAYNE
his Servants.

The principall Comœdians were,

WILL. SHAKESPEARE. RIC. BVRBADGE.
AVG. PHILIPS. IOH. HEMINGS.
HEN. CONDEL. THO. POPE.
WILL. SLYE. CHA. BEESTON.
WILL. KEMPE. IOH. DVKE.

With the allowance of the Maſter of REVELLS.

From BEN JONSON'S FOLIO, edited in 1616, and set up in print while Shakespeare was still alive. The place accorded him in the list of actors, at the end of *The Alchemist*, shows that in his life-time he was placed on an equality with Richard Burbadge.

The Workes of William Shakeſpeare,
containing all his Comedies, Hiſtories, and
Tragedies: Truely ſet forth, according to their firſt
ORIGINALL.

The Names of the Principall Aĉtors
in all theſe Playes.

William Shakeſpeare.	Samuel Gilburne.
Richard Burbadge.	Robert Armin.
John Hemmings.	William Oſtler.
Auguſtine Phillips.	Nathan Field.
William Kempt.	John Underwood.
Thomas Poope.	Nicholas Tooley.
George Bryan.	William Ecclestone.
Henry Condell.	Joſeph Taylor.
William Slye.	Robert Benfield.
Richard Cowly.	Robert Goughe.
John Lowine.	Richard Robinſon.
Samuell Groſſe.	John Shancke.
Alexander Cooke.	John Rice.

From the FIRST FOLIO, edited in 1623 by Shakespeare's fellow-players John Hemmings and Henry Condell, who are themselves included in the list.

Much Ado About Nothing, V. 3. 19:
> Graves, yawn and yield your dead
> — — x — x —

Macbeth, I. I. I:
> When shall we three meet again
> — x x — — x —

Macbeth, I. I. 7:
> There to meet with Macbeth
> — x — — x —

Macbeth, I. 2. 18:
> I'll drain him dry as hay
> — — x — x —

(which the *Clarendon* editors quietly changed into: "I will drain him dry as hay"; Dover Wilson too prints: "I will . . .".)

Macbeth, IV. I. 6:
> Toad, that under cold stone
> — x — x — —

(which in Dyce's edition appears as: "Toad that under the cold stone", while in *The Arden Shakespeare* the suggestion, as "undoubtedly correct", has been made that "cold stone" should be read as "coldest stone".)*

That tendency towards stressing two, or even more, consecutive syllables has not vanished from English poetry, although it had been forgotten for a long time. To quote only one modern poet, T. S. Eliot, there are in his lyrical as well as dramatic diction lines such as these:

from *The Journey of the Magi:*
> And three trees on the low sky
> x — — / x x — —

from the *Four Quartets:*
> Time present and time past
> — — x x — —

---

*Dover Wilson thinks that *cold* is either a dissyllable or the line "lacks a syllable."

Are both perhaps present in time future

x — x x — x x — — x

from *The Family Reunion:*

The cold spring now is the time

x — — — x x —

The slow flow throbbing the trunk

x — — — x x —

Does it seem to go too far to assume that Shakespeare has similar linguistic faculties? and similar artistic aims? Or are we to believe that those lines are nothing but "slovenly metre"?

(B)

The special reason why the text of *Macbeth* shows more four-foot lines than any of the other plays seems to lie in the fact that the Witches have influenced not only Macbeth's actions but also his language, both of which, after all, originate from the same mind.

That drop of poison that enters Macbeth's mind is so potent that throughout the play he continually tries to regain his equilibrium, all the time wavering between "foul and fair", between "ill and good", between "lost and won". Whenever he ponders he weighs up the one against the other, balancing the two scales of wishing it "highly" and wishing it "holily".

In fact, the language of the whole play seems to be infected by that drop of poison. Like a tuning-fork sounded, there is a continuous trembling between Yes and No. The word "double" runs through the whole composition like a figured bass: "double trust"—"double sense"—"double sure". The word is not only actually spoken, but also implied in numerous phrases:

Doubtful it stood . . .

                whence comfort seem'd to come,
Discomfort swells . . .

. . . which grain will grow and which will not . . .

Win us with honest trifles to betray's
In deepest consequence . . .

Cannot be ill, cannot be good . . .

And nothing is, but what is not . . .

              . . . wouldst not play false,
And yet wouldst wrongly win . . .

To be thus is nothing, but to be safely thus . . .

Nought's had, all's spent . . .

Returning were as tedious as go o'er . . .

That keep the word of promise to our ear,
And break it to our hope . . .

It has its deep significance that the Weird Sisters' "foul and fair" is mirrored in Macbeth's first words:

So foul and fair a day I have not seen.

Less obvious but no less significant is the parallelism between the Witches':

When the battle's lost and won

and Duncan's words at the very end of I. 2.:

What he hath lost, noble Macbeth hath won.

With these words the King endows Macbeth not only with Cawdor's title, but also with the treacherous mind of "that most disloyal traitor". The word "win" re-echoes in the phrases "win us . . . to betray us" and in "wouldst wrongly win"—and it reverberates in the Lady's "Nought's had, all's spent".

That weighing-up process has its bearing on Macbeth's diction. It is this struggle for equipoise in his mind that results in that ambling way of expressing himself, as when he says:

> Cannot be ill, cannot be good:
> — x x — / — x x —

or:

> And nothing is, but what is not.
> x — x — / x — x —

It is obvious that a four-foot line with its symmetrical halves is better suited to vacillating thought than the five-foot metre. By arranging the lines so as to obtain normal five-foot iambics the editors interfere not merely with one of Shakespeare's finest subtleties of diction, but also, one might say, with Macbeth's way of thinking.

(1)

Turning to the first of his balancing speeches I propose to arrange it as I think it ought to be arranged; it is the passage I. 3. 130 ff.:

> This supernatural soliciting
> Cannot be ill, cannot be good.
> If ill?
> Why hath it given me earnest of success,
> Commencing in a truth? I am thane of Cawdor.
> If good?
> Why do I yield to that suggestion
> Whose horrid image doth unfix my hair . . .

> ————————————

> My thought,
> Whose murder, yet, is but fantastical,
> Shakes so my single state of man,
> That function is smother'd in surmise,
> And nothing is, but what is not.

After "If ill?" and "If good?" or after "My thought"
I do not mean to have long pauses. (Had Shakespeare
wanted them he would have made the words occupy a
line of their own—and it is probably because he wished
to avoid such pauses that he put the two questions and
"My thought" at the beginning of their respective lines,
which thus give the impression of being six-foot iambics.)
What I mean by putting those words outside the metre
is their function as pegs, so to speak, on which the consequent lines are hung up—similar to those previous cases
(which might typographically be put like this):

> Yes!) As sparrows eagles, or the hare the lion.

and

> So they—) Doubly redoubled strokes upon the foe.

or the line from *The Merchant of Venice*, I. 3. 127:

> Say this:) Fair sir, you spet on me on Wednesday
> last . ..

That those words do stand outside the metrical scheme
is shown by the fact that the lines that follow are ordinary
iambics: we have only to remember that "suggestion" has
four syllables and that, a few lines later, "function" has
three.

The firm and steady rise in the line:

> Shakes so my single state of man,

with its four equally stressed accents almost amounts to
an outcry. After the climax in "man" there is a moment's
pause, as indicated by the comma. In the lines:

> That function is smother'd in surmise,
> And nothing is, but what is not.

we have commas after "surmise" and "is": clearly showing
how the author wishes the lines to be spoken: the first
distinctly brought to its end, the last divided into halves.

The editors, however, have arranged them as follows:

> Shakes so my single state of man that function
> Is smother'd in surmise; and nothing is
> But what is not.

The rhythm is spoiled, the two high points in "man" and "surmise" are levelled down—and once more Shakespeare's diction ignored.

But, it may be asked, is not my arrangement an arbitrary one? In fact, it is that of the Folio.

(2)

In his soliloquy, in III. I. 48 ff., Macbeth begins in the same balancing manner. In the Folio his lines read like this:

Seru. They are, my Lord, without the Pallace Gate.
Macb. Bring them before vs.   *Exit Seruant.*
> To be thus, is nothing, but to be safely thus:
> Our feares in Banquo sticke deepe,
> And in his Royaltie of Nature reignes that
> Which would be fear'd. 'Tis much he dares, . . .

We should keep in mind the existence of such lines as:

> Cannot be ill, cannot be good
> — x x — / — x x —

or:

> And nothing is, but what is not
> x — x — / x — x —

and we should remember that Shakespeare was not unacquainted with the spondaic metre. There is that line in *Hamlet*, III. 2. 270:

> Thoughts black, hands apt, drugs fit, and time
> agreeing
> — — / — — / — — / x — x — x

which, with its three heavy spondees, pictures the stealthy

pace of Lucianus, the murderer. There is á line of similar
purport in *Richard III*, IV. 4. 75:

> Earth gapes, hell burnes, fiends roar, saints pray
> — — / — — / — — / — —

—in short, I think that the lines in question should be
scanned like this:

> To be thus, is nothing, but to be safely thus:
> x x — x — x / x x x — x —
> Our fears in Banquo stick deep,
> x — x — x / — —
> And in his royalty of nature reigns that
> x x x — x x x — x / — —
> Which would be fear'd. 'Tis much he dares . . .
> x — x — / x — x —

The position of "stick deep" and "reigns that" (at the
end, the very climax of their lines) and their heavy pro-
nunciation seems to be far more impressive than in the
editors' arrangement, where they are whittled down to
insignificance:

> Our fears in Banquo
> Stick deep; and in his royalty of nature
> x — x — x — x x x — x
> Reigns that which would be fear'd; 'tis much he
> x — x — x — x — x —   dares . . .

Once more Shakespeare's definite wishes as expressed
in line-division as well as in punctuation have been dis-
regarded—for the mere fetish of "regular" versification.

(3)

III. 2. 4 ff:

Lady M.: Say to the king, I would attend his leisure
          For a few words.

Serv. Madam, I will.   (*Exit*.)
Lady M.: Nought's had, all's spent,
    Where our desire is got without content:

It is a matter of course that the Lady—in the same way as Macbeth himself in the previous instance—waits for a moment until the servant has got away, and then starts a new line. To have it otherwise is completely un-Shakespearian.

The line

   Nought's had, all's spent
   — — / — —

is a line to itself, consisting of two spondees. It is a line of the pattern as that from *Hamlet:*

   Thoughts black, hands apt . . .
   — — / — —

or that from *Richard III:*

   Earth gapes, hell burns . . .
   — — / — —

The words are most expressive. One can almost see the Lady, staring with wide-open eyes into the void, with the worm already gnawing her heart, the words drawn out like sighs of despair: "Nought's ——— had, all's ——— spent", evenly balancing the "nought" against the "all", the "had" against the "spent"— gain and loss, life and death. And all that in four words!

Yet this acme of expressiveness has been treated by the editors as though it were a mere remainder of the Servant's words. They have arranged the lines like this:

  For a few words.
    Madam, I will. (*Exit*.)
      Nought's had, all's spent . . .

(4)

In the following passage (III. 2. 41 ff.) I reproduce the line-division and punctuation of the Folio.

> ere to black Hecate's summons
> The shard-borne beetle, with his drowsy hums,
> Hath rung night's yawning peal,
> There shall be done a deed of dreadful note.

Lady M.: What's to be done?

Macb.: Be innocent of the knowledge, dearest chuck,
Till thou applaud the deed: Come, seeling night,
Scarf up the tender eye of pitiful day,
And with thy bloody and invisible hand
Cancel and tear to pieces that great bond,
Which keeps me pale. Light thickens,
And the crow makes wing to th' rooky wood . . .

(a)

The line:

> Hath rung night's yawning peal
> x — — — x —

is a four-foot verse, complete in itself. If the actor has the imagination to hear the beetles' "drowsy hums" and speaks the next line as if listening to them, enouncing his words slowly, softly stressing each syllable, and, first of all, enjoying himself the truly musical sound, the magical harmony of the four vowels: "rung—night's—yawning—peal"—: the effect cannot fail.

(b)

After the Lady's question: "What's to be done?" the verse is broken off. The pause demands, or is caused by, acting. Macbeth will probably look into her eyes and

think for a moment whether or not he should tell her.
No, he wishes to spare her the pain of uncertainty. With
a smile he shakes his head, and then:

> Be innocent of the knowledge, dearest chuck. . . .

(c)

Also the line:

> Which keeps me pale. Light thickens
> x — x — / — — x

is a four-foot verse. The words with their long vowels
move slowly: "keeps me pale"—a gaze up to the sky:
"Light thickens"—: one can feel the peaceful evening,
growing dark. But then the tempo gets quicker:

> And the crow makes wing to th' rooky wood. . . .

—black and ominous, flapping noisily—one can visualize
the crow flying past—: it is like a Chinese water-colour,
painted in words.

What have the editors done? They have:

ad (a): completed the "defective" line by filling it up:

> Hath rung night's yawning peal, there shall be done
> x — x — x — x — x —

—leaving "night's" unstressed, thus completely spoiling
the rhythm of the line no less than its sound.

ad (b): obliterated the pause by making Macbeth
answer his Lady without a moment's hesitation:

> A deed of dreadful note.
>   What's to be done?
> Be innocent of the knowledge, dearest chuck. . . .

ad (c): Once more they have "corrected" Shakespeare: by lengthening the one line and, at the same time,
shortening the other.

126

Which keeps me pale! Light thickens, and the crow
Makes wing to the rooky wood.

By this process the noun "Light" is left unstressed, which
is a loss. What by that disregard of Shakespeare's intentions has been gained I cannot tell.

(5)

In 1. 7 56 ff. all modern editors, including Dover
Wilson, have the following line-division:

I would, while it was smiling in my face,
Have pluck'd my nipple from his boneless gums,
And dash'd the brains out, had I so sworn as you
Have done to this.
Macb.:   If we should fail?
Lady M.:   We fail!
But-screw your courage to the sticking-place . . .

That looks regular, correct, unsuspicious. Should we
not, however, after what we have seen so far, expect a
pause after "We fail"? In fact, looking into the Folio we
find the lines arranged like this:

And dasht the Braines out, had I so sworne
As you haue done to this.
Macb. If we should faile?
Lady M. We faile?
But screw your courage to the sticking place. . . .

In the modern way of printing verse, the lines would
appear like this:

And dash'd his brains out, had I so sworn
As you have done to this.
Macb.:   If we should fail?
Lady M.: We fail? (————————————)
But screw your courage to the sticking-place. . . .

This arrangement, though the original, did not find favour in the editors' eyes, obviously for two reasons: (a) the line: "And dash'd . . ." seemed to them to be irregular and to have four feet only, and (b) the words "We fail" to be left outside the metrical scheme. Yet the two points prove only that the passage is a veritable gem of Shakespeare's diction.

Is the actress to scan the line like this:

And dash'd the brains out
x — x — x

dropping the "out"? That would not do. Or perhaps like this:

And dash'd the brains out
x — x x —

dropping the word "brains"? Neither, of course. There can be no doubt that every skilled actress will stress both words:

And dash'd the brains out
x — x — —

—and that is exactly the way in which, as he has made it glaringly clear, Shakespeare wishes the line to be spoken. Scanned as he wrote it the line is a five-foot iambus.

And dash'd the brains out, had I so sworn
x — x — — / x — x —

In case a corroborative parallel should be needed I refer to the instance, given in v. (4), also from *Macbeth*:

That would be howl'd out in the desert air
x — x — — x x — x —

The consequent line, divided between the two speakers, is a regular iambus:

As you have done to this.
                                    If we should fail?

Then follows the Lady's exclamation:

We fail?

— —

—and there is the long ensuing pause we have been looking for. With what kind of emotion the two words should
be spoken: with contempt, or anger, or inability to understand, with astonishment, or ridicule, it would be im-
prudent for anybody to say. Nor dare I suggest with
what wordless acting the Lady should fill in the pause.
Whether she ought to shake her head pityingly, unable
to believe in the possibility of so weak a mind, or whether
to look him up and down in amazement, or whether to
grasp him by the arm, no one can say. Nor should anybody try to pronounce on such subtleties of acting. If
the actress gives way to her own emotional urge the
gesture will come by itself; and it will be the right
one. On the other hand, whatever she does, doing it
merely because she is told to, will be wrong and fail to
convince.

(This is why, as it will have been noticed by now, I
always make at least two suggestions when I have to say
where and why a gesture, etc., ought to be made. The
actors are sensitive instruments, in no way easier to play
on than Hamlet's recorder: "though you can fret me, you
cannot play upon me". The producer may help an actor
in producing his, the actor's, emotions, but he should
never try to produce them for him.)

                                    ★

To sum up: I do not believe in the "corruptedness" of
the text of *Macbeth*. On the contrary, I think that the
text of this play has preserved more of its author's
peculiarities of writing than any other play, the reason
being that it has been less interfered with.

The "irregularities" of diction for which Shakespeare has so often been blamed are like those "mazes intricate" of which Milton speaks when he describes the "mystical dance" of the stars; he calls them

> Eccentric, intervolv'd, yet regular
> Then most, when most irregular they seem;
> And in their motions harmony divine
> So smooths her charming tones, that God's own ear
> Listens delighted.

Paradise Lost, v. 623 ff.

XII

"THOU" AND "YOU"

In the normal course Shakespeare's characters say "you"
to each other. They change over to "thou" when they
depart from the level of normal feelings—no matter
whether their emotions rise up or go down to tenderness
or disdain, to passionate love or hatred. The change from
"you" to "thou" and vice versa serves, as it were, as an
emotional barometer.

This is no peculiarity of Shakespeare's. We find in
other writers, too, that "you" and "thou" are of different
emotional temperature. Tamburlaine calls Zenocrate
"you" when he first meets her; as soon as he declares his
love he changes to "thou". Zenocrate, first mistaking him
for a mere shepherd, calls him "thou", but uses the
respectful "you" as soon as she learns he is a "lord".
Nevertheless, there seems to be no fixed rule: she falls
back to "thou", and he, too, is inconsistent: when, at the
end of I. 2., he goes off with her he again says "you".
Abigail, before her death, speaks to Friar Barnardine:
twice she says "you" to him, once "thou", although there
is no change in her emotions. In *Edward the Second* the
King's Niece says to the younger Spenser:

> Spenser, stay *you*, and bear me company,
> For I have joyful news to tell *thee* of. . . .

In fact, neither Marlowe nor, for that matter, Ben Jonson
nor any other of the Elizabethan writers appear to have
been guided by anything like a principle.

With Shakespeare this was different. Not that he
followed any rule or regulation; but his sense of the
theatre was so strong, and to such an extent was he able
to transform himself into his creatures while he created

them, that rise or fall in the emotions of his characters led by itself to "you" being exchanged for "thou" and to "thou" for "you". That being so, we are in a position to watch that change as though it were the swaying hand of the barometer indicating calm or thundery weather.

(1)

In *Twelfth-Night*, III. 1., Olivia addresses Cesario with "you". Having revealed her love and met with a refusal she dismisses the "good youth". No sooner, however, has Viola turned to leave than Olivia is overpowered by her feelings: "Stay!" she cries. There follows a pause—the word "Stay!" stands outside the metrical scheme—a pause apparently filled in by Olivia's coming up to Viola. And now, transported by her ill-applied passion, she addresses the young gentleman with "thou":

> I prithee, tell me what thou thinkst of me?

Cold-shouldered by "him" she returns at once to "you". Shortly afterwards, however, her passion once more gets the better of her and again she cannot help addressing Cesario with "thou".

(2)

In *Much Ado About Nothing*, I. 1. 215 ff., Don Pedro addresses Benedick with "thou": cracking jokes with him he treats him as his equal. Then, however, he sends Benedick on an errand, and with that he returns to the formal "you": now it is the inferior to whom he speaks. The actor should conform to that change of address by a change in his attitude: having first dropped his princely bearing, he should resume it when he returns to "you".

(3)

In II, *Henry IV*, II. 4., Doll says "you" to Falstaff as long as she is annoyed with him: "You muddy rascal . . hang yourself", etc. As soon as she changes her attitude she changes to "thou": "Come, I'll be friends with thee, Jack, thou art going to the wars . . .", etc. Later, however, she changes again. As long as she sits on his knee she says: "I kiss thee . . I love thee better . . ." But then the Prince appears, and at once she tries to lay distance between herself and the muddy rascal: "How, you fat fool, I scorn you".

In the same scene Prince Hal as usual calls Falstaff "thou". But when Falstaff calls him a drawer, the Prince, falling in with the joke, answers as a drawer and, accordingly, says "you" to him: "Very true, sir; and I come to draw you out by the ears".

(4)

In *King Lear*, IV. 5. 19 ff., Regan tries to make Oswald surrender to her Goneril's letter addressed to Edmund. He refuses. She tries once more:

> Why should she write to Edmund? Might not you
> Transport her purposes by word? Belike,
> Some things—I know not what—I'll love thee
> much—
> Let me unseal the letter.

It is an unequivocal proposal: this harlot princess is prepared to bestow her favours on him in payment for that letter. Oswald—what a character!—rejects the offer, with the result that Regan, genuine daughter of Eve that she is, jumps back from it at once, as though she had not said anything at all, and returns to "you".

What a gem of acting! If the actress understands the meaning of that change she will no doubt find several ways of showing what Regan wishes to hint at—only, as soon as she is snubbed once more, to drop the whole matter as if making and retracting such an offer were the most natural thing in the world.

Does my suggestion go too far? Does it show too great a depravity in that woman? Yet she is not only able to stab a man in his back and kill him at a moment's instance as she does in III. 7.; she is undoubtedly also an adulteress. In themselves' her words: "I'll love thee much" might pass as harmless, meaning mere gratitude or some permissible favour: it is the change in her form of address that makes all the difference. Before and afterwards she says "you"; in between comes that sudden "I'll love thee"—even: "I'll love thee much"—: that, I should think, makes it unmistakable.

(5)

One might almost say that the change from "you" to "thou" always indicates physical nearness, no matter whether that means an embrace or a friendly pat or, as in the case of Othello, strangling.

When, in I. 5., we see Macbeth and the Lady together for the first time, she greets him with:

Great Glamis! worthy Cawdor!
. . . .
Thy letters have transported me . . .

It is obvious that they embrace. When, however, they come to the matter in question, Duncan's arrival and what is to follow, she uses "you". In I. 7., as long as she sneers at him, using the words "afeard" and "coward", she says "thou". He shows anger—and she returns to "you": she still speaks with great violence, yet from now on without any jeer.

In III. 2., Macbeth first says "you" to his wife. Then there is a change:

> O, full of scorpions is my mind, dear wife:
> Thou know'st, that Banquo and his Fleance lives.

If the actor takes the author's hint that lies in the change to "thou", he will probably put his arm round her and lower his voice, speaking intimately, perhaps even whispering. Up to then he had spoken of his sorrows in general; now he speaks, if darkly, of his plan. She understands at once:

> But in them, nature's copy's not eterne.

He sees that she is at one with him, and feels relieved: "There's comfort yet . . ."—and that feeling of alleviation leads him to that lyrical passage with "night's yawning peal". He keeps addressing her with "thou"—a fact that should induce the actors to remain physically near to each other throughout the rest of the scene.

I think I am justified in saying that the use Shakespeare makes of that change from "you" to "thou" and vice versa—a change that often enough amounts to a veritable stage-direction—is a peculiarity of his diction.

XIII

PUNCTUATION

IT seems improbable that it will ever be possible to ascertain Shakespeare's own punctuation. Too numerous are the plays that have, before they were printed, been tidied up either by theatrical scriveners or by some corrector at the printing house or, finally, by the compositors themselves. Our first task would be to exclude from the examination all the "corrected" texts in order to narrow down the search to those plays that have not been interfered with, or at least not too much—a thing easier said than done.

Dr. Percy Simpson, in his book *Shakespearian Punctuation*, makes use of a different approach: he widens the field of scrutiny by examining also the works of Ben Jonson, Drayton, Barnfield, and others. His aim evidently was not so much to find out Shakespeare's, but Shakespearian, punctuation, i.e. a punctuation normally used by the Elizabethans. Yet in an age that had not yet developed general rules of grammar, or spelling, still less rules of punctuation, to look for something even approaching a system seems a chimerical undertaking. In those days people strutted about displaying bright colours in their doublet and hose, wearing feathers in their hats and rings in their ears: everyone who wanted to show his importance sported his own fashion and style not only in his clothes but in everything else—and something of that multifarious liberty and gay individualism is mirrored in the Elizabethan punctuation.

Moreover, even if we restrict our investigation to those plays of which we may assume with any measure of probability that they show at least partly Shakespeare's own punctuation we might still find it difficult to make out any cut and dried system in it. We cannot assume that in default of a general rule he should have invented and carefully thought out an individual rule for himself, and still less can we assume that he should have stuck to it. Great masters do not allow their hands to be bound, not even by the chains they themselves have forged.

All the same, it would be equally wrong to assume that Shakespeare used his punctuation marks without any discrimination. The evidence as drawn from the best-preserved texts of the Folio tends to show that he was in the habit of choosing in each individual case just that mark he thought would best meet, not any principle, but the theatrical need of the moment. Accordingly we should not so much look for an explanation why he uses just this and no other mark, but rather try to find out why he uses any mark at all.

(A)

Comma and Question-mark

Needless to say, Shakespeare did not invent what might be called the "more-than-grammatical use" of punctuation, as little as he invented the blank verse. And yet it may be said that the way he makes use of the means of punctuation is largely his own. What with others is merely a method of expressing their thought as clearly as possible becomes in his hands a sensitive instrument with which to indicate theatrical subtleties, especially of declamation.

(1)

In the passage from *Macbeth*, I. 3. 133 ff., he uses question-marks:

If ill?)   Why hath it given me earnest of success,
Commencing in a truth? I am thane of
Cawdor.
If good?) Why do I yield to that suggestion . . .

But the passage does not differ very much from that in *Hamlet*, I. 2. 86 ff., where Hamlet speaks of his "inky coat":

Seems, madam? Nay, it is: I know not "seems":
. . . .
These, but the trappings, and the suits of woe.

The comma after "These" has the same function as a question-mark: "[As to] these [garments]? [They are] but the trappings and the suits of woe."
All editors omit that comma.

(2)

Hamlet, III. 2. 270 ff.:

Thoughts black, hands apt, drugs fit, and time
agreeing:
Confederate season, else, no creature seeing . . .

The comma after "else" has disappeared from all editions. But how telling that comma is! Lucianus, before pouring his poison, looks round to make sure that no one watches him (no conscientious murderer would omit such circumspection) and only then is he in a position to state: "No creature seeing". The comma stands for a question-mark: "else?—no creature seeing."

If grammar excludes the comma, why not print a query? To print no mark at all is certainly a step away from Shakespeare, not nearer to him.

(3)

II, *Henry IV*, IV. 2. 107/8: Hastings returns with the news that his army has dispersed. Westmoreland replies:

> Good tidings, my lord Hastings, for the which,
> I do arrest thee, traitor, of high treason.

A sudden change from amity to the "block of death". Certainly Westmoreland raises his voice in "for the which" and pauses a moment—a moment of tension— before he pronounces the arrest. At least he is advised to do so—by the comma after "which". But this comma is omitted in all modern editions.

(4)

In *Measure for Measure*, II. I. 18 ff., Angelo remarks:

>   I not deny
> The jury passing on the prisoner's life
> May in the sworn-twelve have a thief, or two
> Guiltier than him they try . . .

The editors omit the comma after "thief". By doing so they make Angelo say that among the jury there may be a sprinkling of thieves—"one or two". If, however, taking Shakespeare's hint, one makes a pause after "thief", be it ever so short, the words: "or two" amount to: "or (even) two". It is not the same whether one says: "Among twelve there may be one or two criminals" or: "there may be a criminal, perhaps even two."

(5)

In *Hamlet*, I. 3. 99 ff., Ophelia is questioned by Polonius about her relations to Hamlet. According to the Folio she replies:

> He hath my Lord of late, made many tenders
> Of his affection to me.

The editors have omitted the comma after "late". Is it really meaningless?

Ophelia, naturally, is sensitive to her father's inquisitiveness. She hesitates: "He hath, my lord, of late . . ."
—what is she to say? Which expression should she use?
—and chooses an awkward one: ". . . made many tenders of his affection to me", thus giving Polonius the opportunity of letting his wit gallop around the word "tender". In that comma lies her hesitation, her looking round for an expression that would not be too outspoken. A modern author would probably write: "He hath, my lord, of late . . . (*pause of hesitation*) . . . made many tenders of his affection to me".

(6)

A few lines further on (101) we have a similarly ungrammatical and illogical comma. Having been scolded by her father for taking Hamlet's "tenders for true pay", Ophelia replies:

> My Lord, he hath importun'd me with loue,
> In honourable fashion.

Why should Ophelia speak of Hamlet's "honourable" intentions spontaneously? Would a young woman such as she touch on that aspect of herself? Certainly she would do so only by way of replying to doubt or reproach. I submit that that is actually what she does. She first says only: "—he hath importun'd me with love"; Polonius, however, taking the phrase in an ambiguous sense, turns towards her with some gesture of "How?—what?", whereupon she makes haste to defend herself by adding the qualification: "—in honourable fashion!"

140

The editors have done away with that comma. But it is not the same whether Ophelia states as a matter of fact: "—he hath importun'd me with love in honourable fashion" or whether she defends her maiden honour: "—he hath importun'd me with love . . . (no, no!) in honourable fashion!" How much livelier the dialogue becomes by such little touches of the producer's hand!

(7)

In *Twelfth-Night*, II. 2., Viola is told that she had left a ring with Olivia. Malvolio urges her to take it back; but Viola does not know of any ring, and she answers:

> She tooke the Ring of me, Ile none of it.

That is how the Folio prints the line. The editors, however, have changed the comma into a semicolon, thus turning the first half of the sentence into a statement. Yet it is a question. Astonished as she is, Viola says as it were: "[What did he say? that] She took the ring of me? [that is not true]: I'll none of it."—and thus, as a query, it should be punctuated.

(8)

In *Julius Cæsar*, III. 2. 84 ff., Antony, in his oration, first tells the citizens:

> The Noble Brutus
> Hath told you Cæsar was Ambitious.

There is no comma: the sentence is a mere statement. Later on, however, Antony repeats the sentence three times, and each time there is a comma after "sayes":

> Yet Brutus sayes, he was Ambitious.

141

The contents of his words is the same as before; their use, however, is now different. Having stated the fact, Antony now plays with it. Three times he uses it to hit out at Brutus. The words are intended to sound like: "Yet [what is it] Brutus says? [He says] he was ambitious."

Shakespeare apparently wishes the actor to raise his voice in "says" and then to stop for a short moment; to indicate this he put those three commas. To replace them by question-marks would perhaps go one step too far; but at least the three commas should be left untouched. The editors have blotted them out.

(9)

The line in *Macbeth*, II. 2. 62:

> Making the Greene one, Red.

does not mean that "the green one", i.e. the sea, would become red, but that the green colour of the sea would become "one red", i.e. one entirety of red. Shakespeare could not add, beneath the line, an indication how he wanted it to be pronounced:

> Making the green one, red
> — x x — — —

(for this line, too, is a four-stressed verse); nor can I see how that could be done in modern print either.

(10)

In *Othello*, I. 1. 40 ff., we have an ungrammatical question-mark; Iago says:

> Now, Sir, be iudge your selfe,
> Whether I in any iust terme am Affin'd
> To loue the Moore?

The sentence begins with: "be judge yourself" and, according to the rules of grammar, an imperative cannot end with a question-mark. But the doubt seems to be justified whether Iago has ever heard about those rules (?). And even if he had, one might wonder whether he would be prepared to alter the highly expressive manner of his talk(?). For him the sentence: "whether I am affined to love the Moor" is a query, he puts it as a query—and as a query it ought to be printed.

(11)

The passage goes on:

Rod. I would not follow him then
Iago: O Sir content you.
　　　I follow him, to serue my turne vpon him.

Here the editors have changed the full stop after "content you" into a semicolon. By doing so they have not only interfered with the punctuation but, in a sense, also with the line-division. After: "O Sir content you" there is a pause, as indicated by the gap in verse, before Iago goes on: "I follow him . . .". By putting that semicolon, however, the editors have tried to divert the actor's attention from that pause, telling him as it were: "Go on with the speech. There is a gap in the verse, but never mind; simply slip to the next line, that's all." But surely that cannot be the right way of dealing with Shakespeare's intentions?

So far Iago has spoken of his hatred for Othello; now he goes—or pretends to go—one step further: he draws

his "friend" into his confidence. He "discloses" to him
. . . what? Not very much: he only makes some dark
allusions, revelling in sententious generalities. All the
same, he tries to give his gullible companion the impression that he is laying his heart open to him; and he does
so not only with words, but also with profuse gestures of
intimate friendship. (Among Shakespeare's characters
it is probably Iago who more than anyone else
accompanies whatever he says with prodigious and
most expressive gesticulations. Not only his tongue is
voluble, but his whole body seems to take part in his
fluency.)

After "O Sir content you" Iago probably looks round
to make sure that no one is listening, perhaps he takes
his friend's arm, leading him a few steps aside, and only
after some such humbug, and certainly in a changed voice,
he "reveals" to him confidentially:

> I follow him, to serve my turn upon him.

But how can the actor be expected to find out the meaning of such a pause and to comply with Shakespeare's
intentions if so much is done to obliterate them?

(12)

The next line:

> I follow him, to serve my turn upon him

has a comma after "him". All the editors have omitted
it; but how much poorer the diction is without
that comma!

The comma stands for something like: "yes, but only".
If the actor is told that the line means: "I follow him
[all right, but merely] to serve my turn upon him", he

will know at once how to make that meaning clear: by a
twinkle of his eyes, a grimace, by a raised finger, or whatever he may find fitting.

★

Of that comma—the comma of a type that I should
like to call "the raised-finger type"—there are innumerable
instances. Sometimes such a comma may actually indicate a raised finger; often, however, it may merely imply
a short pause, a raised eyebrow, a twinkle of the eye, a
poking in the rib, etc.

Macbeth, III. 2. 38:
> But in them, nature's copy's not eterne

Twelfth-Night, I. 3. 60:
> You mistake knight: Accost, is front her

I, *Henry IV*, I. 2. 208:
> The vertue of this Iest will be, the incomprehensible
> lyes

II, *Henry IV*, Induction, 15:
> Rumour, is a Pipe

II, *Henry IV*, IV. 3. 110:
> The second propertie of your excellent Sherris, is,
> the warming of the Blood

Hamlet, IV. 2. 30:
> The King, is a thing ————

King Lear, I. 2. 17:
> Our Fathers loue, is to the Bastard Edmond

Othello, II. I. 324:
> Knaueries plaine face, is neuer seene, till vs'd.

Othello, V. 2. 355:
> And smoate him, thus.

In all these and countless other cases the editors have

145

thought we could do without the comma. Perhaps we can. Yet what would we say if in a modern edition of Beethoven's Symphonies all "piano" and "forte" signs were to be omitted?

(B)

The Colon

In Shakespeare's usage each one of the punctuation marks has to serve several purposes: the comma is sometimes used as a query, sometimes as a dash, sometimes it indicates a pause. The query stands often as an exclamation mark. The full stop functions sometimes as an exclamation mark, sometimes as a dash—and so it goes on.

Considering the great versatility of Shakespeare's punctuation marks it is little wonder that the colon, too, is not restricted to one function only. Its first and probably original task seems to have been a logical one, that of summing up. That seems to have led naturally enough to that of contrasting or connecting one line of thought with the next one, much as a bridge contrasts, but at the same time connects, the two banks of a river. Finally, since summing up as well as linking together are frequently accompanied by a gesture, or even demand one, the colon often seems to have no other purpose than to indicate a gesture.

(1)

In *Macbeth*, II. 3., in the Porter's soliloquy, we have five colons:

> Here's a knocking indeede: if a man were Porter at
> Hell Gate, hee should haue old turning the Key. (a)

. . . that hang'd himselfe on th' expectation of
Plentie: Come in time . . . (b)

. . . could not equiuocate to Heauen: oh come in,
Equiuocator (c)

. . . for stealing out of a French Hose: Come in
Taylor . . . (d)

. . . Ile Deuill-Porter it no further: I had thought
to haue let in some of all Professions . . . (e)

The colons (a) and (e) are more of the logical type,
although it may be that the Porter accompanies them
with a gesture, perhaps that of shaking his head; their
chief task, however, is that of connecting one trend of
thought with the next. The colons (b), (c), and (d) on the
other hand seem to be hardly more than indications of a
gesture, be it a bow, a movement of his arm, or a friendly
beckoning with his hand, with which the devil-porter
invites and welcomes the newcomers to his establishment.

(2)

Shortly afterwards Macduff asks:

Is thy Master stirring?
Our knocking has awak'd him: here he comes.
Lenn. Good morrow, Noble Sir.

The colon after: "awak'd him" cannot be a logical one
—and the editors have changed it into a semicolon. Yet
are we to take it as meaningless? I think it stands for a
gesture. Macduff asks about Macbeth. There follows a
gap in the metre, probably caused by the Porter, who
silently draws Macduff's attention to his master's approach.
Macduff sees him coming—"Our knocking has awak'd
him"—and, turning back towards Lennox (this move-

147

ment is indicated by the colon), he adds: "Here he comes".
In point of fact, it is Lennox who says: "Good morrow.
noble sir."

(3)

A few lines later Macbeth says:

> The labour we delight in, Physicks paine:
> This is the Doore.

There is no logical link between the two sentences. The
colon indicates nothing but a gesture—that with which
Macbeth points towards the door. The editors put a full
stop in the place of the colon. Yet why should a sign,
meaning "gesture", be eliminated?

(4)

In *Twelfth-Night*, II. I. 30 ff., Antonio asks Sebastian's
permission to go with him; Sebastian refuses. Antonio
asks him to let him at least know whither he is bound;
another refusal. A third time Antonio asks: ". . . Let me
be your seruant". To which Sebastian replies:

> . . . desire it not. Fare ye well at once, my bosome
> is full of kindnesse, and I am yet so neere the
> manners of my mother, that vpon the least occa-
> sion more, mine eyes will tell tales of me: I am
> bound to the Count Orsino's Court, farewell.

Ant. The gentlenesse of all gods go with thee:
I haue many enemies in Orsino's Court,
Else would I very shortly see thee there:
But come what may, I do adore thee so,
That danger shall seeme sport, and I will go. (*Exit*)

Sebastian, after three refusals, suddenly discloses where he is going. But is it really so sudden? After "mine eyes will tell tales of me" there is a colon—and this colon indicates both a pause of deliberation and a gesture. Sebastian is struggling with himself; evidently he makes a few steps towards his exit, then turns half round (the gesture indicated by the colon), flings his words back over his shoulder, and runs off.

Antonio is left alone. After his first line we find a colon, indicating another mental process, yet at the same time demanding a gesture. He turns to leave the stage (in the direction opposite to that of Sebastian's exit): the gesture demanded by the colon. But then an idea stops him: "How much I should like to follow him! But can I?"

> I haue many enemies in Orsino's Court,
> Else would I very shortly see thee there:

After "there" another deliberation: "Can I risk it? Is it not too dangerous for me?"—with the result:

> But come what may, I do adore thee so,
> That danger shall seeme sport, and I will go.

The actor, if he takes up the two hints given him by Shakespeare himself, will presumably after his first line hesitatingly either turn away or even start to leave; then, stopping, speak to himself: "I have many enemies . . ."; yet after "see thee there", with a quick movement, he will turn round and look in the direction where Sebastian left: "But come what may . . ."—and then definitely and determinedly follow him.

★

A short list of colons may follow, all of them gathered from previous instances, colons indicating gesture:

L

Macbeth, I. 2. 5:

    'Gainst my captivity: Hail, brave friend

                [turn towards the Captain]

Macbeth, I. 4. 27:

    Welcome hither: [Duncan embraces Macbeth]

Othello, I. 3. 193:

    Come hither, Moor: [Othello comes nearer]

Othello, III. 3. 383:

    Nay, stay: [walk] thou shouldst be honest.

Hamlet, II. I. 84:

    To speak of horrors: [deep breath] he comes before

                               me.

Measure for Measure, II. 2. 45:

    Give't not o'er so: [Lucio turns Isabella towards
    Angelo] to him again, entreat him

(5)

Finally an instance from *Twelfth-Night*, interesting for an additional reason. In III. 4. 38 ff., when Malvolio, in yellow stockings and cross-gartered, is asked by Maria: "How do you, Malvolio?", he answers, according to the accepted text:

    At your request! yes; nightingales answer daws.

In the Folio, however, Malvolio's reply, divided in two lines, reads like this:

    At your request:
    Yes Nightingales answere Dawes.

Why did the compositor, instead of continuing the line, leave that large space after "request"? Obviously because he found that gap in the manuscript. If so, has the gap any meaning? I submit that the colon stands for a gesture, and apparently for a rather elaborate one:

Malvolio looks Maria up and down contemptuously before, turning his back on her, he finishes her off with the devastating remark that he, a nightingale, could never answer a ridiculous daw.

The additional interest lies in the evidence, as shown in this instance, that pauses are indicated not only in verse, but sometimes also in prose passages. If further evidence should be needed we only need read on a little until we reach the lines 67 ff., which in the Folio appear as follows:

Ol. Ile come to him.
    Good Maria, let this fellow be look'd too. Where's my Cosine Toby. . . .

After "I'll come to him" there is a big gap, indicating a pause. In this pause Olivia, making for the exit, evidently takes Maria aside and withdraws with her from Malvolio before she, certainly in a confidential voice, gives order that cousin Toby should look after "this fellow".

The editors print the text without any interruption, thus obliterating a pause which both author and compositor were careful enough to make.

(6)

In *Measure for Measure*, II. I. 60 ff., we read in modern editions:

Ang. Go to: what quality are they of? Elbow is your name? why dost thou not speak, Elbow?
Pom. He cannot, sir: he's out at elbow.

Of course every actor will after "your name?" pause, waiting for Elbow's reply. The remarkable thing is that in the Folio that pause is indicated, one might almost say, is made, by a gap in the text. There we find:

Ang. Goe to: What quality are they of? *Elbow* is your
  name?
Why do'st thou not speake *Elbow*?
Clo. He cannot Sir: he's out at Elbow.

Other instances can be found in the same play, in
Macbeth, in *King Henry IV*, and elsewhere.

(7)

In *Troilus and Cressida*, III. I. 146 ff., Pandarus tries
to divide his flattery between Paris and Helen. At the
same time, however, he has serious business with Paris
which, in a silent understanding, they keep hidden from
Helen. Within a dozen lines (prose lines) there are three
interruptions, indicated by broken-off lines: the two men
speak in private. Helen notices their having a secret, and
remarks: "He hangs the lip at something", meaning
Paris; she wishes Pandarus to tell her what is going on,
but does not receive an answer.

Pan. Is this the generation of loue? Hot bloud, hot
  thoughts, and hot deedes, why they are Vipers, is
  Loue a generation of Vipers? (——————————)
  Sweete Lord whose a field to day?
Par. *Hector, Deiphoebus, Helenus, Anthenor*, and all the
  gallantry of *Troy*. I would faine haue arm'd to day,
  but my *Nell* would not haue it so. (——————————)
  How chance my brother *Troylus* went not?
Hel. He hangs the lippe at something; you know all
  Lord *Pandarus?*
Pan. Not I honey sweete Queene: I long to heare how
  they sped to day: (——————————)
  Youle remember your brothers excuse?
Par. To a hayre.
Pan. Farewell sweete Queene.

152

I submit that without the stage-business, indicated by the broken-off lines, the passage can scarcely be understood. The pauses as shown in the Folio text are a great help. In all the modern editions, however, they have been omitted.

(C)

The "Nought"

In addition to the usual marks there is one, completely foreign to modern compositors, which might be called the "Nought". I mean the mark that consists in the absence of any mark at all. The normal function of the "nought" is that of a long dash, indicating a long pause, filled in by special acting.

(1)

Love's Labour's Lost, V. 2. 725: Marcade arrives with the sad news of the French King's death:

Marc. I am sorrie Madam, for the newes I bring is heauie
      in my tongue. The King your father
Qu. Dead for my life.
Marc. Euen so: My tale is told.

After "The King, your father" the messenger hesitates. The Princess (already called the Queen) looks at him, notices his grave bearing, and understands: "Dead . . .".

(2)

Antony and Cleopatra, V. 2. 321:

1 *Guard.* Where's the Queene?
Char. Speake softly, wake her not.
1 *Guard.* Cæsar hath sent
Char. Too slow a Messenger.

The soldier, at the sight of the dead Queen, breaks off. Only after a pause, filled in with emotion, Charmian, soliloquizing, remarks: "Too slow a messenger." I do not believe that she interrupts the man, which is what the editors evidently assume: they print the passage as though the line, falling in halves, were one sentence:

Cæsar hath sent—
　　　—too slow a messenger.

(3)

Love's Labour's Lost, v. 2. 164: "The Boy with a speech" declaims his poem; he has memorized it badly.

Pag. That euer turn'd their eyes to mortall views.
　　　Out
Boy. True, out indeed.

Here it is certainly impossible to assume that Boyet interrupts the Page. The boy "is out", he fumbles for the next words and cannot remember them. There must be a pause.

(4)

Also in *Hamlet*, I. 5. 2, we cannot assume that Hamlet interrupts his father's Ghost. After all that long preparation and delay, after leading his son away from the others, at last the Ghost speaks. It is unthinkable that Hamlet should break into the apparition's speech: there must be a pause—and there it is, indicated by the "nought" after "Mark me".

Ham. Where wilt thou lead me? speak; Ile go no further.
Gho. Marke me
Ham. I will.

There can be no doubt that the first words the Ghost

utters have a tremendous emotional impact on Hamlet. Previously, for three nights the apparition had been seen, but had not spoken, despite efforts to make it speak. This night, too, as long as the others were present it had refused to speak. Hamlet himself had asked, nay, implored it to speak, but its only response was a repeated beckoning. Is it more than a mere spectre, a "fatal vision"? Perhaps it is only "a false creation, proceeding from the heat-oppressèd brain". But now the apparition opens his lips and Hamlet hears—what does he hear?— his father's never-forgotten voice. His father is dead and buried; yet here he stands and speaks to his son. And it *is* his father, for there is his voice.

What would I do if my dead father's ghost were to appear and speak to me? Would I drop to my knees? Would I be choked with tears? I do not know. But I know for certain that my heart would rise into my throat and for some time I should not have an answer ready. Shakespeare has indicated that pause of Hamlet's being overwhelmed with emotion. And yet, what do we find in all the editions? The line has been "regularized"— with the result that Hamlet sen. and jun. answer each other tit for tat; every hint at a pause has been obliterated.

> Mark me.
> I will.
> My hour is almost come. . . .

Surely the plays could be edited in a manner more helpful to actors and producers?

All the same, just as in the case of the other punctuation marks, the "nought", too, has to serve more than one purpose. There are instances where it indicates not a pause, but an interruption, as in the following examples:

(5)

Much Ado About Nothing, III. 3. 16 ff.: Dogberry is fond of talking, especially if he can do it himself:

> ... but to write and reade, comes by Nature.
> *Watch 2.* Both which Master Constable
> *Dogb.* You have: I knew it would be your answere:

(6)

Love's Labour's Lost, V. 2. 380:

> *Ros.* This proues you wise and rich: for in my eie
> *Ber.* I am a foole, and full of povertie.

That Berowne actually interrupts the lady is shown by Rosaline's immediate reproof:

> *Ros.* But that you take what doth to you belong,
> It were a fault to snatch words from my tongue.

In these and many other instances the "nought" simply takes over from the comma, which also is often used to indicate interruption, as in the following double instance.

(7)

Love's Labour's Lost, I. I. 226 ff.:

> *Ferd.* Peace,
> *Clow.* Be to me, and euery man that dares not fight.
> *Ferd.* No words,
> *Clow.* Of other mens secrets I beseech you.

The editors print Ferdinand's words as "Peace!" and "No words!", thus obliterating the fact that the Clown really "snatches the words from his tongue". The passage would be better arranged like this:

156

Ferd. Peace . . .
Clow. . . . be to me, and every man that dares not fight.
Ferd. No words . . .
Clow. . . . of other men's secrets, I beseech you.

It appears impossible indeed to try to put the punctuation marks of the Folio into any sort of system. The best we can do is to take each of them individually, and not allow ourselves to be disturbed at seeing that for a certain purpose there has in that case that mark been used, and in another case, another. The only important fact is that a punctuation mark has been inserted at all; which, is less decisive. What the mark really means we have to find out in each case separately.

(D)

Tempo

In a musical work the composer indicates not only "piano" and "forte" but also the tempo in which he wishes the piece or a certain part of it to be performed. So does Shakespeare. There can be no doubt that the passage from *Hamlet:*

Thoughts black, hands apt, drugs fit, and time
agreeing

— — / — — / — — / x — x — x

is to be spoken slowly, and that on the other hand certain sentences in *Much Ado About Nothing* ought to flit by like darts:

Thy wit is as quick as the greyhound's mouth: it catches. ˉ

x — x x — x x — x — / x — x

Will you, then, write me a sonnet in praise of my beauty?

— x x — x x — x x — x x — x

In these instances, however, the tempo lies in the rhythm itself: in the one case the line lurches along as though in felt-boots, in the other it is a game of battle-dore and shuttlecock. Yet there are instances where the tempo not of single sentences but of whole passages is indicated—indicated by punctuation.

Even in recent books one can still read that one par-ticular play is more "heavily punctuated" than another. Yet I should think it is not so much the sum total of punctuation marks that . counts, but their distribution among the characters. One individual character's part may be said to be more "lightly" or more "heavily" punctuated than another's—and even then we have to take care not to be rash in our assessment since it occurs sometimes that one character's part may in this passage be "heavily", in another passage "lightly" punctuated.

I have to confess, however, that I do not know what the terms "heavy" and "light" punctuation really mean. Are the marks to be counted or weighed? Shakespeare uses an accumulation of marks on one occasion for slowing down, on another for quickening the tempo. In my opinion the distinction should not be between "heavy" and "light" punctuation, but between "accelerando" and "ritardando".

(1)

The beginning of Othello's speech before the Senate (1. 3. 76 ff.) is in the Folio pointed like this:

> Most potent, grave, and reverend signiors,
> My very noble, and approv'd good masters;
> That I have ta'en away this old man's daughter,
> It is most true: true, I have married her;
> The very head, and front of my offending,
> Hath this extent; no more. Rude am I, in my
>   speech . . .

In these six lines the editors have changed one semicolon into a comma; one colon and one semicolon exchanged for each other; and four commas omitted. Thus they have accelerated the tempo, despite the fact that Shakespeare in this case uses a punctuation that may indeed be called "heavy", because by that means he wishes to characterize Othello's speech: slowly and heavily getting into its stride.

(2)

As long as Shylock is in normal temper his speeches are punctuated in the normal way. In his tirade against Antonio, e.g. (I. 3. 107 ff.):

Signior Antonio, many a time and oft . . .

we find (in the Folio) that the sentences are divided by semicolons, colons, queries, and full stops. Apparently he is keeping his emotions well under control. As soon, however, as he gets nearer his "merry sport", i.e. the pound of flesh, his speech accelerates: nothing but commas are used.

Why look you how you storm,
I would be friends with you, and have your love,
Forget the shames that you have stain'd me with,
Supply your present wants, and take no doit
Of usance for my moneys, and you'll not hear me,
This is kind I offer.
Bass.: This were kindness.
Shy.: This kindness will I show,
Go with me to a notary, seal me there
Your single bond, and in a merry sport
If you repay me not on such a day,
In such a place, such sum or sums as are
Express'd in the condition, let the forfeit
Be nominated for an equal pound

> Of your fair flesh, to be cut off and taken
> In what part of your body it pleaseth me.

And again:

> Pray you tell me this,
> If he should break his day, what should I gain
> By the exaction of the forfeiture?
> A pound of man's flesh taken from a man,
> Is not so estimable, profitable neither
> As flesh of muttons, beefs, or goats, I say
> To buy his favour, I extend this friendship,
> If he will take it, so: if not adieu,
> And for my love I pray you wrong me not.

Shylock's, and his author's, intentions are obvious: he wants to let his murderous offer appear as involving no risk at all; he underlines the harmlessness of the whole thing by the rapidity of his speech—like a hawker who wants to overwhelm his prospective buyer's suspicions. (The editors have slowed down the tempo by exchanging nine commas for: one exclamation-mark, one full stop, three semicolons, and four colons—and by adding two dashes.)

(3)

Again, when standing before the Duke's Court, and conducting his lawsuit, Shylock speaks like a man in full command of himself: his speeches show all sorts of stops. In III. 1, however, enraged by his daughter's escape, he talks in a way that hardly brooks any stop at all.

> Nay, that's true, that's very true, go Tubal, fee me an officer, bespeak him a fortnight before, I will have the heart of him if he forfeit, for were he out of Venice, I can make what merchandise I will: go Tubal, and meet me at our synagogue, go good Tubal, at our synagogue Tubal.

This torrent of speech has been slowed down : five
commas have been exchanged for four semicolons and one
full stop. No one would dare to put an "andante"
where Mozart himself has said "prestissimo".

(In Shakespeare's usage a comma, if put between otherwise independent sentences, does not separate but connects—in contrast to the other stops, all of which produce
a gap between the sentences. That function of the comma
seems to explain the meaning of the word "comma" in
Hamlet, v. 2. 42:

Claudius's letter contains

> An earnest conjuration from the king,
> As England was his faithful tributary,
> As love between them like the palm should flourish,
> As peace should still her wheaten garland wear,
> And stand a comma 'tween their amities . . .

The meaning seems to be that the two countries should
remain linked together—as sentences are linked together
by commas.)

(4)

In *Hamlet*, iv. 5. 98 ff., there is noise outside, the King
calls for his Switzers, and a Messenge˙ rushes in:

> Save yourself, my lord.
> The ocean (over-peering of his list)
> Eats not the flats with more impitious haste
> Than young Laertes, in a riotous head,
> O'erbears your officers, the rabble call him ˙ ˙.
> And as the world were now but to begin,
> Antiquity forgot, custom not known,
> The ratifiers and props of every word,
> They cry choose we? Laertes shall be king,
> Caps, hands, and tongues, applaud it to the clouds,
> Laertes shall be king, Laertes king.

The punctuation of the passage is an indication of the tempo with which, in his agitation, the Messenger speaks. The editors have inserted: one full stop, one exclamation-mark, and two semicolons, thus interrupting repeatedly where Shakespeare clearly says: "No interruption, please!"

(5)

Ophelia's report on Hamlet's visit (II. I. 75 ff.) falls into two parts: first eight and then fourteen lines. In the first part she describes how Hamlet arrived: disturbingly, frighteningly. She speaks presto; the eight lines contain twelve stops: one colon and eleven commas.

But then, her first flush of alarm gone, she regains her composure: there is a considerable rallentando. In fourteen lines there are twenty stops: fourteen commas, but then three semicolons, one colon, and two full stops. The scene she depicts is slow, as if filmed with a slow-motion camera: "held me hard—hand o'er his brow—perusal—long stay'd he so (— — x —) —at last, a little shaking —waving—and to the last—": this description, quiet, long-drawn-out, should be rendered with the same slowness.

In both parts of the speech the "tempo giusto" has been clearly indicated by the author, who was meticulous enough to use here six heavy stops (brakes as it were) and there nothing but commas.

(6)

In *King Lear*, I. I. 146 ff., Kent does his best to bring his old master back to reason. In the punctuation of the Folio the passage reads like this:

Let it fall rather, though the fork invade
The region of my heart, be Kent unmannerly,
When Lear is mad, what wouldst thou do old man?
Think'st thou that duty shall have dread to speak,
When power to flattery bows? To plainness
                        honour's bound,
When majesty falls to folly, reserve thy state,
And in thy best consideration check
This hideous rashness, answer my life, my judg-
                               ment:
Thy youngest daughter does not love thee least,
Nor are those empty-hearted whose low sound
Reverbs no hollowness.

Needless to say, this accumulation of commas is no
slovenliness, as the editors apparently thought. The
punctuation shows (and is intended to show) the frantic
haste and violence with which Kent endeavours to bring
Lear to his senses. By "regularizing" the punctuation
the editors have been successful in making Kent's speech
appear more logical and dignified; at the same time, however, they have done away with a vital characteristic of
this particular passage: its breathlessness and emotional
energy.

Players are just such judges of what is right, *as Taylors are of what is* graceful. *And in this view it will be but fair to allow, that most of our Author's faults are less to be ascribed to his wrong judgment as a Poet, than to his right judgment as a Player.*

ALEXANDER POPE,
Preface to The Works of Shakespear,
1725.

In the First Folio there are four poems of commendation. The last of them reads as follows:

WEE wondred (Shake-speare) that thou went'st so
soone
From the Worlds-Stage, to the Graues-Tyring-
roome.
Wee thought thee dead, but this thy printed worth,
Tels thy Spectators, that thou went'st but forth
To enter with applause. An Actors Art,
Can dye, and liue, to acte a second part.
That's but an Exit of Mortalitie;
This, a Re-entrance to a Plaudite.

I. M.

The author of this poem was James Mabbe, a translator of Spanish literature and Fellow of Magdalen College, Oxford. He, among those contributors, was the only one who thought of Shakespeare as an actor. The others, Ben Jonson, Hugh Holland, and Leonard Digges, speak of the "beloued Author", the "Scenicke Poet", the "deceased Authour"; none of them even mentions their friend's histrionic abilities. And yet, Shakespeare would not be half the man he is had he not been so "excellent in the quality he professes", as Henry Chettle has said of him.

164

It was John Aubrey who said of Ben Jonson: "Now B. Johnson was never a good actor." There needs no ghost come from the grave to tell us this. Jonson's plays, and still more so his innumerable footnotes, show clearly their author's scholarship; but no one with any stage-practice would ever think that they have been written by an actor.

With Shakespeare's plays it is a different matter. If nothing at all were known as to who wrote them our first guess would be that their author must have been a theatrical man. Wherever one turns, whatever one examines, be it his punctuation, his way of dividing the lines, his policy of pauses, or any other aspect of diction, it seems impossible not to realize that no one but a professional actor—and one of the first rank only—could have written those plays.

In their case it is evident that the author was his own first actor, in the sense that he, single-handed, performed each of the parts—and not only the parts: he performed, or rather (to use the modern term) he produced, the whole play while he was writing it; or, more exactly: what he put down in words was the outcome of those one-man rehearsals. The real first-nights of Shakespeare's productions took place on a private stage that, small though it was, was nevertheless the most grandiose the world ever had: the stage behind his eyes.

Thus it is that those texts have come into existence not as material for subsequent production, but as the product of production. Stage-directions, therefore, advice to the actors, and other additions such as in the normal way of theatrical practice the producer would work out in his stage-book in order to make the best of the text he has to deal with—all that has by that individual author been tried and weighed and tested beforehand: during those silent rehearsals.

It is that double personality that accounts for Shake-

M

speare's unique achievements—the fact that he was not only a great poet but no less great an actor; not only a great playwright but also a great producer. In these two strains we have the warp and waft that, inseparably interwoven, make the tissue of his plays the matchless marvels they are.

Yet while we admire the tapestries, the final fabric of those double endeavours, can we hope to draw conclusions from the literary texture to the histrionic skill that went into its making? Can we hope to revive something that together with its owner died and was buried so long ago? Is it true that

> An Actors Art,
> Can dye, and liue, to acte a second part—?

Shakespeare did not write any footnotes: no introductory descriptions are given; no explanations, put between brackets, elucidate the text; no stage-directions in the modern sense of the word are added. All he has to say he says in the text itself: there he gives everything necessary; what he does not give is not necessary.

True, by putting those punctuation marks, by making those various gaps and metrical pauses, he seems to say —and often enough—: "Here pause for a moment!" or: "Make a gesture there!". But what the gesture ought to be or with what kind of emotion the pause should be filled, he never says. When we recall the elaborate stage-directions we find in the plays of Bernard Shaw's the question obtrudes itself, "Which is the better method of dealing with the actors?"

First, actors are artists and should be treated as artists. Author and producer may appeal to their intellects, but neither of them should try to interfere with their emotional reactions. In these, the actor must be completely free. Try to make him feel in a way that is yours but not his, because it has not been generated in his own heart, and the result will be false and unconvincing. How can he hope to translate to his hearers an emotion he does not feel himself?

When Macbeth (I. 7.), in a last feeble attempt to escape his own plan, sounds the warning:

> If we should fail?

his Lady answers:

> We fail?

Two words; but in how many ways, with how many nuances is it possible to pronounce them! Astonishment, anger, unbelief, contempt—shouting, whispering, hissing, laughing, jeering: each of these expressions, and many others as well, might be the right one, if really felt and genuinely produced. Now, for the author to write down one of those expressions would not be the best thing to do: his direction, be it a thousand times the right one for himself, might run counter to the genuine feelings of an individual actress—perhaps one of genius—and then, in this case, his direction would no doubt be wrong. Such things may happen; for intellects may be brought to work in parallel lines, but feelings sometimes fly off at a tangent. And if we imagine similar authoritative directions spread over the whole play, directions to Macbeth, Duncan, Banquo, etc., would not the players feel cabined, cribbed, confined, bound in? You cannot fetter a dancer's feet without spoiling his performance; and you should not try to fetter an actor's heart.

There is yet another consideration. In matters of art, to give less than all is often more than to give all. At the beginning there was the command: "Let there be light!" Yet the smaller creators, at least the great among them, especially when their days grew late, got gradually down to another, more modest command: "Let there be twilight!" The old Rembrandt, the old Goethe, the old Beethoven, the old Michelangelo, they all learned to spread over their later productions a diffuse dimness, a silver veil that covers up all less important bywork and incidentally throws the main features into a mysterious high-relief.

This slight indistinctness in their maturer work is not due to any lack of clarity in the artist himself, but to his conviction that his work, finished though it be, must remain incomplete as long as it is not given his audience's collaboration: their emotional co-ordination and concurrence in receiving his work. Their imagination must be kindled—and he has realized that the more he says to explain his own work the more is he in danger of extinguishing that flame in his onlookers, his readers, his actors. "Bilde, Künstler, rede nicht!", says Goethe. "Go on creating, man of art; don't talk!" And somewhere else he says: "A poet's production, the more inscrutable it is and to the intellect impalpable, the better."

Bernard Shaw does not share that opinion. As the profound thinker he is and as the improver of mankind he wishes to be, he endeavours to bring light into every dark corner. That is why he is not content to write his plays and leave the rest to producers and actors, but makes all those additions to elucidate his texts. (A tendency he has in common with Ben Jonson, whom he recalls in other ways as well.) "Elucidation" is the word on his banner. And since he is also, or perhaps chiefly, a philosopher and sociologist, many of his plays are not self-contained entities, mere works of art, but components of a greater design: steps towards a better world, a world of higher intellectualism. That is the final end for which he strives with all his means, of which his plays are one part only.

Shakespeare had no such aims. Betterment of mankind: did he ever think of that? Social criticism? That he left to Ben Jonson. And as to poetry—of course he was a poet; he could not help being one, as little as a giant ever ceases being a giant, even when crouching on the floor. But only on rare occasions, if ever, did he strive after poetry for its own sake. Whenever poetry happens to occur in his plays it is put in as yet another means to attain what to him was the higher aim, his only aim: to write good plays, i.e. plays with good parts for actors.

Now, which is a good part? That with the finest poetry? or is it that that demands the highest intellect? I should think it is that part that contains the strongest emotional tension, varied through change of gear. Romeo: suffering from unrequited love; falling in love; at the height of love; separated from his love; new hope; utter despair; yearning for reunion with his love. Macbeth, all the time struggling: with his own ambition—with his own fear—his own imaginings—his better self—his own despair: fighting from the beginning to the end his worst enemy, himself. To create emotions and over again emotions, a maximum both in intensity and variety, that is Shakespeare's true ambition. Everything else: poetry, credibility of events, historic truth, realities of time, poetic justice, and many other matters, all that is to him of secondary consideration. The emotion is the thing—and emotion is expressed not merely in words but in pauses also, just as music consists not merely in notes, but in notes and rests. Language is but the vehicle for emotions; the plate for the food, not the food itself.

The words have come down to us; their emotional contents can be made out. But how are we to gauge the right emotions with which to fill in those many pauses of wordless acting?

"Language," Dr. Johnson said, "is the dress of thought." As to Shakespeare's characters, however, I would say that language is more than their dress; it is their skin. Their speeches are sloughs, as it were—or, to use a more human simile: they are like those mysterious holes that were found when Pompeii was excavated. First, no one knew the origin and nature of those cavities in the otherwise compact ground, and many of them were destroyed by the unthinking pickaxe. Soon, however, the diggers learned to pour plaster into the openings; when the filling had hardened they carefully removed the surrounding soil, and thus obtained the casts of people who, buried under the rain of cinder and fallen to dust long since, had left in the covering ashes the form of their bodies. They themselves are dead; yet in the near-by museum, behind glass, their plaster copies can be seen, stretching their limbs in fantastic attitudes. We can imagine their screams of mortal fright when we gaze at their fear-distorted faces and horror-stricken gestures, retained through so many centuries by the shape of a hole in the earth.

Of Shakespeare's means of histrionic expression much has been buried under the dust of time. But let the actor find those broken-off lines, those gaps and pauses, and he will know how to fill them—with his own feelings. The actor's contribution to the art of the stage, the ever-renewing pulse of his emotions, has remained unchanged.

APPENDIX

SOME PROBLEMS OF TRANSLATING SHAKESPEARE

WHILE working through the proof copy of the present book the idea occurred to me that the reader might be interested in reading more, and in a more coherent form, about the problem of translating Shakespeare.

The subject is fascinating and much, no doubt, could be said about the true aims a translator is to pursue, about the means at his disposal, and the difficulties he has to overcome. For obvious reasons, however, I have to content myself with giving a mere summary; and so I shall deal with only two aspects of the problem—rhythm and sound—choosing only such instances as may, reflected in the mirror of translation, throw back some light on the original itself. And without any theorising I propose to dive straight into the matter.

(1)

On p. 52 I have referred to *Macbeth*, IV. 3. 194:

                    but I have words
That would be howl'd out in the desert air . . .
x — x — — x x — x —

The line combines the problem of sound, that of the deep and drawn-out vowels "howl'd—out", with that of rhythm, the clashing of the two stressed syllables. Dorothea Tieck (in "Schlegel-Tieck") renders the line as follows:

> Doch ich habe Worte—
> O, würden sie in leere Luft geheult . . .
> x — x — x — x — x —

The problem has not been solved, neither in sound nor rhythm, because the subtlety of diction had not been noticed. In my version the line reads:

> Doch ich hab Worte—
> Dürft' ich sie aus-heulen in leere Luft . . .
> — x x — — x x — x —

The rhythm, with the two clashing syllables, is imitated, and "aus-heulen" lends itself to being pronounced in the same lugubrious way as "howl'd out".

(2)

On p. 122 the line 270 from *Hamlet*, III. 2, has been quoted:

> Thoughts black, hands apt, drugs fit, and time agreeing
> — — / — — / — — / x — x — x

Its rhythm, with the three spondees at the beginning, depicts the slow and stealthy pace with which the murderer Lucianus, poison in hand, slinks up to his sleeping victim. The slow and uncanny tread of the line is unusual, and clearly intended to be so. Schlegel translated the line as though it were just another blank-verse:

> Gedanken schwarz, Gift wirksam, Hände fertig . . .
> x — x — / x — x / — x — x

But surely if there is a line in Shakespeare where what he says is at least equalled in importance by how he says it, it is this line. What in this case the translator has to consider first is the rhythm: the stealthy pace must be rendered. My version reads:

Herz giert, Hand strebt, Gift schwält, die Stunde neigt
sich . . .

— — / — — / — — / x — x — x

(3)

Juliet, in III. 5. 208 ff., says to the Nurse.

How shall that faith return again to earth,
Unless that husband send it me from heaven
By leaving earth? comfort me, counsel me!
x — x — (x) — x x — x x

Juliet concludes the last line, after a gap in verse, with
two dactyls, crying out for help. Schlegel, sticking to
the tenet of regular versification, regularized what he
thought was faulty metre: he filled in the gap and made
the whole line a normal five-foot iambus:

Wie soll die Treu zur Erde wiederkehren,
Wenn sie der Gatte nicht, der Erd entweichend,
Vom Himmel sendet? Tröste, rate, hilf!
x — x — x / — x — x —

Yet by this smoothing-out process a characteristic expression of Juliet's mentality has been smoothed out also:
her impatience or, better to say, her impetuousness, which
she, still the half-child she is, displays in so many ways
and on so many occasions. In that line, Schlegel's Juliet
implores the Nurse; Shakespeare's, demands. Transferred
into action or gesture: Schlegel's Juliet raises her hands
in supplication; Shakespeare's stamps the ground in
vexation. Alter a character's rhythm, and you alter his
or her mind.

In my translation the passage reads:

Wie kann mein Eid vom Himmel wiederkehren,
So lang mein Gatte nicht, entflohn in Himmel,
Ihn niederschickt? Tröst mich doch, hilf mir doch!
x — x — (x) — x x — x x

(4)

On pp. 47 ff., various lines have been quoted, showing "irregularities" in their rhythm; here I give a few of their counterparts in my version:

(a) The grey-ey'd morn smiles on the frowning night . . .
x — x — / — x x — x —
Der blaue Tag lächelt der düstern Nacht . . .
x — x — / — x x — x —

(b) This but begins the woe others must end.
— x x — x — / — x x —
Manch schwarzer Tag folgt nach, einer wird's enden.
— x x — x — / — x x — x

(c) And to the last, bended their light on me.
— x x — / — x x — x —
Und bis zuletzt ruhte ihr Licht auf mir.
— x x — / — x x — x —

(d) To giue them Seales, neuer my Soule consent!
x — x — / — x x — x —
Das Siegel "Tat"—nie lass es zu, mein Herz!
x — x — / — x x — x —

(e) Words without thoughts, neuer to Heauen go.
— x x — / — x x — x —
Wort ohne Sinn niemals zum Himmel dringt.
— x x — / — x x — x —

(5)

On p. 157 I have quoted two sentences from *Much Ado About Nothing*. The intention was to show their tripping rhythm.

(a) The line:

Will you, then, write me a sonnet in praise of my
beauty?

— x x — x x — x x — x x — x

has been rendered by Wolf Graf Baudissin ("Schlegel-Tieck") as follows:

> Wollt Ihr mir dafür auch ein Sonett zum Lobe meiner Schönheit schreiben?

The contents of the sentence has been rendered, but not its rhythm. Baudissin, it appears, held the opinion that in prose, rhythm does not matter. My version tries to copy the rhythm as closely as possible:

> Schreibt Ihr mir dann ein Sonett zum Preis meiner Schönheit?
>
> — x x — x x — x — x x — x

(b) Another line, also from *Much Ado About Nothing* (I. I. 151):

> You always end with a jade's trick: I know you of old.
>
> x — x — x x — — / x — x x —

This has been rendered by Baudissin as follows:

> Ihr müsst immer mit lahmen Pferdegeschichten aufhören; ich kenne Euch von alten Zeiten her.

With sentences like these needlessly drawn-out and heavily plodding, how is the actress to reproduce Beatrice's crispiness of diction? Especially her parting dart, threatening Benedick with more combats to come: "I know you of old" (x — x x —) falls completely flat when rendered with: "Ich kenne Euch von alten Zeiten her" (x — x — x — x — x —). My translation reads:

> Ihr macht immer Schluss wie ein bockiges Pferd; ich kenn Euch schon lang!
>
> x x — x — x x — x x — / x — x x —

(6)

One more example, the last, of rhythmic subtlety; it has been quoted on p. 38. Here, however, I am going to refer also to the line following next.

> For in that sleep of death, what dreams may come,
> When we have shuffled off this mortal coil,
> Must give us pause. There's the respect
> x — x — / (x —) / — x x —
> That makes calamity of so long life:
> x — x — x x x — — — —

It is impossible to assume that the pause after "pause" should have come about by chance or negligence—and there is nothing for the translator to do but to reproduce it. Schlegel once more regularized and thus overturned a signpost set up by Shakespeare's own hand.

> Was in dem Schlaf für Träume kommen mögen,
> Wenn wir den Drang des Ird'schen abgeschüttelt,
> Das zwingt uns still zu stehn. Das ist die Rücksicht,
> x — x — x — / x — x — x
> Die Elend lässt zu hohen Jahren kommen.
> x — x — x — x — x — x

My version reads:

> Im Todes-Schlaf, was wir da träumen mögen,
> Wenn wir den Trug des Irdischen abgeschüttelt,
> Das lässt uns zaudern:—das ist die Scheu,
> x — x — x / (— x) / — x x —
> Die trübste Mühsal so lang leben lässt.
> x — x — x — — — x —

The third line with its gap and rhythm speaks for itself. In the last line "so" is so placed that it must necessarily be stressed. The effect of "*so* long" is much stronger than that of "so *long*": the longevity in "so long life", the words equally stressed (— — —), is not only spoken of, but almost audible in the three long and elongated syllables. In my version, too, the "so" is accented, and the words "so lang leben" lend themselves to being pronounced in exactly the same way as the original words.

(7)

In v. 2 of *A Midsummer-Night's Dream* Puck is for the
first time serious. He has now the task of conjuring up
the darkness of night, and he does so, other means missing,
by means of words.

> Now the hungry lion roars,
> And the wolf behowls the moon . . .

For the first time he speaks slowly, using deep and dark
vowels. Schlegel translated the lines as follows:

> Jetzt beheult der Wolf den Mond,
> Hungrig brüllt im Forst der Tiger . . .

The night is spoken of, but is not given; the words fail
to sound of night. High and piercingly sharp vowels such
as in "Jetzt" and "Tiger" are out of place. They might
do well in a description of a morning in spring, but they
go badly with the stillness of midnight. In my version
I have tried to accumulate long and dark syllables:

> Nun, vor Hunger brüllt der Leu
> Und der Wolf beheult den Mond;
> Nun, zur Ruh auf karger Streu,
> Schnarcht der Pflüger, müdgefrohnt.

(8)

Othello bids farewell to his soldiership. The lines
(III. 3. 347 ff.) have the function of a "Last Post"—the
General in Othello is dead—and they should sound like a
bugle-call. Repeatedly the syllables clash (as in "shrill
trump", in "ear-piercing fife", etc.) and the whole passage,
though broken in syllables and words, is a trumpet aria
of one unbroken line.

> Oh now, for ever
> Farewell the tranquil mind; farewell content;
> Farewell the plumed troop, and the big wars,
> x — x — x — / x x — —
> That make ambition, virtue! Oh farewell,
> Farewell the neighing steed, and the shrill trump,
> x — x — x — / x x — —
> The spirit-stirring drum, th' ear-piercing fife,
> x — x — x — / (x) — — x —
> The royal banner, and all quality,
> x — x — x / x — — x x
> Pride, pomp, and circumstance of glorious war:
> — / — / x — x x x — x —
> And O you mortal engines, whose rude throats
> x — x — x — x / x — —
> Th' immortal Jove's dread clamours counterfeit,
> x — x — — — x — x x
> Farewell: Othello's occupation's gone.

It is beyond anybody's reach to reproduce in any other language the immortal music of these lines, so unique in their mixture of onomatopoetic consonants and full-sounding vowels. Yet I hope it will be seen from my version that I have not been deaf to the harmony of the passage, and that I have honestly toiled, not to do real justice to it, which is impossible, but at least to pay homage to the master whose art of linguistic expressiveness is truly the Eighth Wonder of the World.

> O, jetzt, für immer
> Fahr wohl nun, Herzensruh, fahr wohl, mein Glück!
> Fahr wohl, wehender Helmbusch, Krieg und Kampf,
> In dem der Ehrgeiz triumphiert—lebt wohl!
> Leb wohl, du wiehernd Ross, grell schmetternd Horn,
> x — x — x — / — — x —
> Du Trommel, die den Mut rührt, schrill Gepfeif,
> x — x x x — — / — x —

Stolz ragendes Panier and Hochgepränge,
— — x x x — x — x — x
Pracht, Pomp und Herrlichkeit glorreichen Kriegs—
— — x — x x — x x —
Und oh, ihr, Todesmörser, deren Schlund
x — — — x — x x x —
Des ewigen Zeus Getöse dröhnend nachahmt,
x — x x — x — x — x — —
Lebt wohl—Othellos Tagwerk ist getan!

(9)

A passage similarly great is that in which Macbeth
(in IV. I. 50 ff.) demands of the Witches that they should
prophesy to him. In his rage he heaps curse upon curse:
he is prepared to let the midnight hags bring down on
mankind whatever disaster they like, if only they will
disclose to him his future. His words, rising higher and
higher, surge on like a tidal wave, until the peak is reached
in the word "sicken". In this high-pitched sound—a
splashing crest of foam—the wave breaks—and the next
word begins with a full-throated "a": "Answer me . . ."

> Though you untie the winds and let them fight
> Against the churches: though the yesty waves
> Confound and swallow navigation up:
> Though bladed corn be lodged, and trees blown down,
> Though castles topple on their warders' heads:
> Though palaces and pyramids do slope
> Their heads to their foundation: though the treasure
> Of nature's germens tumble all together,
> Even till destruction sicken: answer me
> To what I ask you.

In this case the translator must reproduce not only that
sweeping surge but also, or rather first of all, the climax

to which that sweep is piling up: he must crown the passage with that sharp and high-pitched peak that Shakespeare reaches in "destruction sicken".

> Mögt ihr den Sturm entfesseln, dass er wütend
> An Kirchen rüttelt, dass der Wogenschwall
> Die Schiffe einschluckt in den tiefsten Schlund,
> Dass er das Korn in Schmutz fegt, Bäume umbläst—
> Lasst Burgen poltern auf der Wächter Haupt,
> Paläste, Pyramiden ihre Häupter
> Vor der Zerstörung beugen, lasst den Born
> Der kreissenden Natur in Wüstheit wirbeln,
> Bis die Vernichtung siecht—: antwortet mir,
> Was ich euch frage!

(10)

From the passage just quoted and from their own boasts (in I. 3) we know that the Witches in *Macbeth* are wind hags. And as such they introduce themselves in the first scene—not, indeed, by what they say, but by the sound of what they say.

> When shall we three meet again?
> In thunder, lightning, or in rain?

In the first line we have several descriptive elements combined: (*a*) the two consecutive high "ee" in "three meet"; (*b*) their length; (*c*) the fact that the two syllables clash and are equally stressed; and (*d*) the still longer drawn-out "ai" in "again", repeated in "rain".

> When shall we three meet again?
> — x x — — x ————
> In thunder, lightning, or in rain?
> x — x — — / x x ————

We should not forget that the audience in the Globe

Theatre had not read the play before they went to see it. For them, those three creatures were completely unknown. The spectators were in no way prepared, right at the beginning of the first scene, to be suddenly confronted with supernatural beings. True, the three, half men, half women, showed a strange make-up: they looked "So wither'd and so wild in their attire"; but that was all. As they had to enter in broad daylight, with no artificial night around them, with no wind-machine, nor any other of the modern stage-devices, it cannot have been easy to let them appear as "more than mortal". One device, however, the author-producer had at his disposal: his language.

If we reproduce the first line as it is meant to be, chanting it in a high voice, raising it still higher in "three meet", and in "again" slowly coming down as if in a long whine, the effect will be that of a sharp whiff blowing down from some highland heath.

In "Schlegel-Tieck" the two lines have been rendered as follows:

Sagt, wann ich euch treffen muss:
In Donner, Blitz oder Regenguss?

The short and low vowels in "treffen muss" fail to reproduce that wailing sound. In my version I have at least tried to conform to Shakespeare's intentions:

Wann woll 'n wir drei uns wiedersehn?
In Donner, Blitz, im Windeswehn?
— x x — x — x ————
x — x — / x — x ————

Of course, "Windeswehn" (blowing of the wind) is no equivalent of "rain"; but certainly, in this case, more important than a literal translation is the reproduction of the sound.

And as they have come, so they go: "fair————"
—"air————":

Fair is foul, and foul is fair,
Hover through the fog and filthy air.
— x — / x — x ——————
— x x x — x — x ——————

—a high-pitched whistle—wheee-ee————and they have
gone.

★

Yet for all a translator may strive and endeavour;
however faithfully he may serve his master; whatever
technique he may develop, the result will always be as
though one looked at a Rembrandt picture through a
piece of coloured glass, be it green or red or yellow:
certain colours will disappear, other shades will be upset
—in a word, the original symphony of vocals and consonants, their innate magic, will be destroyed.

Goethe said once:

> Translators are panders who extol the attractions
> of a half-veiled beauty: with all their exertions they
> only kindle in us a longing for the original.

Bitter reward, indeed, after decades of toil and trouble
to be called a pander! How I should like to contradict
the Old Heathen! But alas,—at least in the case of
Shakespeare—he is right.

INDEX

INDEX